ADVANC_ _ _ _ _ _ _

M000194535

"Millennial talent experts Joan Snyder Kuhl and Jennifer Zephirin tackle this thorny issue with much-needed clarity and finesse. Through compelling research, stories, and narrative, *Misunderstood Millennial Talent* provides an invaluable look into what the invisible majority of Millennials—the Ninety-One Percent—really need and want. An essential read that belongs on the desk of every leader as the people agenda and Millennials have to be the focus of every leader."

—Kirk Kinsell, CEO and President of
Loews Hotels and Resorts

"An enjoyable and insightful read that provides up-to-the-minute practical advice, whether you're already seeing an increasing shift in Millennials to management roles or looking to increase awareness about managing them and attracting more young talent to your company. Kuhl and Zephirin home in on the most pressing issues—and cogent solutions—for global employers looking to the future of their workforce and leadership."

—Steve Fry, SVP, Human Resources and Diversity,
Eli Lilly and Company

MISUNDERSTOOD MILLENNIAL TALENT

THE OTHER NINETY-ONE PERCENT

MISUNDERSTOOD
MILLENNIAL
TALENT

THE
OTHER
NINETY-
ONE
PERCENT

JOAN SNYDER KUHL
JENNIFER ZEPHIRIN
FOREWORD BY SYLVIA ANN HEWLETT

CENTER
FOR TALENT
INNOVATION

This is a Center for Talent Innovation Publication

A Vireo Book | Rare Bird Books
453 South Spring Street, Suite 302
Los Angeles, CA 90013
rarebirdbooks.com

Set in Minion
Printed in the United States

10 9 8 7 6 5 4 3 2 1

Publisher's Cataloging-in-Publication data

Names: Kuhl, Joan Snyder, author. | Zephirin, Jennifer, author.
Title: Misunderstood Millennial talent : the other ninety-one percent / Joan
Snyder Kuhl ; Jennifer Zephirin ; foreword by Sylvia Ann Hewlett.
Series: Center for Talent Innovation.
Description: First trade paperback original edition. | A Vireo Book. | New
York [New York] ; Los Angeles [California] : Rare Bird Books, 2016. | Includes
bibliographical references and index.
Identifiers: ISBN 9781942600992
Subjects: LCSH Generation Y—Employment. | Generation Y—Attitudes. |
Organizational behavior.| Success in business. | Intergenerational relations. |
Work ethic. | Globalization. | BISAC BUSINESS & ECONOMICS / Workplace
Culture | BUSINESS & ECONOMICS / Organizational Development.
Classification: LCC HF5549.K84 2016 | DDC 658.3—dc23

To the amazing thought leaders who have been at the heart of this research:

Linda Hartman-Reehl
Barbara Keen
Rosemarie Lanard
Frances G. Laserson
Nancy Testa
Karyn Twaronite

PROJECT TEAM

Project Lead
Sylvia Ann Hewlett, Founder and CEO

Quantitative Research
Laura Sherbin, CFO and Director of Research

Pooja Jain-Link, Senior Research Associate

Charlene Thrope, Research Associate

Qualitative Research
Melinda Marshall, EVP and Director of Publications

Anna Weerasinghe, Fellow

Production
Deidra Mascoll, Senior Research Associate

Isis Fabian, Research Associate

Catherine Chapman, Research Associate

Communications
Tai Wingfield, SVP and Director of Communications

Silvia Marte, Communications Associate

CONTENTS

FOREWORD xi

PART ONE: THE NINE PERCENT xvii

1 Can't Work with Them, Can't Work without Them 3

2 Who is Flighty? 13

PART TWO: THE OTHER NINETY-ONE PERCENT 17

3 The Investment Imperative 19

4 Intellectual Growth and Challenge 27

5 Rewarding Professional Relationships 35

6 What the Ninety-One Percent Actually Values 49

7 Millennial Women—Empowered on the Outside, Left Wanting on the Inside 71

8 Older Millennials—The Lost Generation 83

PART THREE: THE ASIA-PACIFIC IMPERATIVE 91

9 China 95

10 Hong Kong 99

11 India 105

12 The Philippines 109

13 Singapore 115

PART FOUR: SOLUTIONS 121

ENDNOTES 141

METHODOLOGY 155

ACKNOWLEDGMENTS 157

INDEX 171

FOREWORD

When I arrived at Cambridge University as an eighteen-year-old freshman, I saw opportunity unfurl at my feet like a red carpet. In the late 1960s, barriers to higher education were falling, and women and minorities were stampeding the gates of the professions, no longer content to be secretaries and clerks. It felt to me that in this brave new world, nothing could trip me up—neither my gender nor my modest background. I could not have been more wrong.

My first term as a student at Cambridge University was rough, and, as it turned out, my problems had much more to do with class than gender. I had grown up in a working class family in the coal mining valleys of South Wales and spoke English with a thick Welsh accent. My classmates at Cambridge, on the other hand, had attended elite private schools (Eton, Harrow, Cheltenham Ladies) and spoke impeccable "Queen's" English.

In class-conscious England, my South Wales accent indicated I was from the lower echelons of society. I dropped my aitches, talked about "our mam," and said "ta" instead of "thank you." Back in the 1970s, these colloquialisms were not regarded as charming or cute. Indeed, my first week at Cambridge I overheard my tutor describe me to a colleague as "uncouth"—a memory that still makes me wince.

At bottom, my accent signaled that I was uneducated or "ill-bred" (to use a particularly demeaning English term). And in a sense I was. At age eighteen, my main extracurricular activities were child minding (I had five younger sisters) and cooking (it was my responsibility to whip up the family evening meal). I had very little knowledge of the world. My father occasionally brought home a local tabloid called the *Western Mail* but didn't see the point of spending hard-earned money on buying a national newspaper, so I knew next to nothing about current affairs. Our household boasted a motley collection of nineteenth-century novels, courtesy of my mother, who loved the Brontë sisters, but outside of that I was not well-read. I'd never been to the theater, shopped at a high-end store, or traveled abroad. We spent family vacations in a trailer park in West Wales. As a result, I had no small-talk skills or cocktail patter. It wasn't a personality thing—I was friendly and outgoing. I was tongue–tied because I didn't have anything to talk about in my new milieu. I had no way of joining in conversations about, for instance, the Tory leadership struggle, the skiing season in Austria, or the latest in bell-bottom jeans. I had spent the summer before college working in the local municipal laundry rolling hospital sheets. Hardly the stuff of Cambridge "small talk"!

My fellow students weren't openly rude or hostile—after all, they were "well-bred" young people—but they kept their distance. I wasn't on the invitation lists for sought-after freshman parties, and I found it impossible to penetrate the cozy circles that dominated the interesting clubs. I remember being the awkward, ignored outsider at the Cambridge Union, the university-wide debating society.

I soon realized that to survive and thrive I needed to strip myself of my accent and lose the most obvious of the class markers that set me apart from my peers. By January of that first year I had embarked on a transformation. I started with voice and speech—which were, after all, how I betrayed my background. I couldn't afford elocution lessons or a voice coach, so I bought a tape recorder and spent long hours listening to, and then attempting to copy, the plummy voices on BBC Radio. I favored newscasters on the BBC World Service since they spoke a particularly clear and neutral form of the Queen's English. It took at least two years, but eventually I nailed it. In addition to fixing my accent, I set about elevating my conversation so that it reflected the caliber of my thinking rather than my class status. I subscribed to the *Guardian* and the *Times Literary Supplement*, and bought cheap tickets to the local arts theater. By the time I graduated I was trying out my newfound cultural and political fluency on a slowly expanding circle of more sophisticated friends.

Looking back at this journey, I have mixed feelings. Sure, I needed to improve my grammar—everyone needs to speak the language they work in well. I also needed to become more fluent in the ways of the world. But did I need to lose my regional accent? I suspect not. My new modulated tones cut me off from my origins and created distance from my family. My parents in particular were hurt that I felt compelled to deny where I came from. I discovered that surmounting the class barrier can be more complicated than hurdling gender bias.

I share these details of my background and my early career journey to underscore how much I identify with today's Millennials—many of whom come from financially-constrained backgrounds. Galloping inequality has hit this generation hard. As we see in this study, the yawning gap between the privileged few (9 percent of the Millennial cohort) and the struggling many (91 percent of the Millennial cohort) is as big and as unforgiving as it was in the UK of my childhood—literally speaking. Income inequality has tripled in the US since the 1970s, and in 2016 the US is as polarized, and as unequal, as class-conscious Britain. The majority of Millennials do not conform to the self-involved stereotypes sensationalized by the media. They do not hop from job to job, because they lack the financial safety net to support such a journey. They cannot afford to take an unpaid internship because they need to start paying down a heavy load of college debt. They haven't summered in the Hamptons and they haven't been coddled by helicopter parents. As a result, they have grit galore. And for employers who offer financial and job security, they have fabulous sticking power.

But here's what they haven't got: networks, subject matter expertise, and soft skills. They may be tech-savvy (those at the younger end of the spectrum), but they're not acquiring the depth and breadth of skills they will need to grow beyond their roles. Not only do they lack connections: they're not building the relationships critical to getting their work done, extending their reach, and progressing in their organizations. They're hard-pressed to find advocates and don't know to cultivate sponsors. They're in dire need of international exposure—given the global nature of business and the new norm of virtual teaming, and of leadership development, as the majority of those over thirty are already occupying management roles.

Talent specialists aren't investing in Millennials because they see them as job-hoppers on whom investment is wasted, or as talent that's too young to warrant development. Yet the vast majority of Millennials are not only sticky: they are the bench strength for leadership. A tidal wave of exiting Boomers leaves a gap that Generation X cannot fill. And because they are the most diverse generation ever to be college-educated, Millennials are also the talent pool with the potential to at last change the face of leadership in corporate America.

As an employer of Millennials, I am acutely aware of both sides of this equation. Millennial talent at the Center for Talent Innovation and Hewlett Consulting

Partners represent the intersections of gender, socio-economic class, race, and LGBT identities, making them attuned to the demographic trends and market needs that define our organizational mission. They come from some of the best schools in the country, and they're impassioned to put that education to work. Yet to step into leadership, they need to close their skill gaps and broaden their networks; they need us to invest in their intellectual growth and foment more rewarding relationships.

I'm committed to making that investment. While there is always the possibility that these young hires will walk out the door, I have found—and our research shows—that investment begets loyalty, particularly in Millennials whose socioeconomic backgrounds dispose them to make the most of every opportunity. I make the investment because our success, like yours, depends on harnessing and developing the skills, insights, and inclusive-leader behaviors that they bring. I make the investment because they are the future of my organization, just as they are the future of yours. And insofar as they are on track to fulfill the vision of diverse leadership that we all hold dear, none of us dare skimp on their development. Millennials are indisputably in charge of our legacies; let us make sure we develop them so that they deepen and drive these legacies well.

—Sylvia Ann Hewlett

PART ONE: THE NINE PERCENT

1

Can't Work with Them, Can't Work without Them

When Renée* was tapped to join the market research team for a project on Millennials with one of her firm's biggest clients, she was thrilled. As a Millennial herself, she looked forward to sharing her insights and showcasing her value to both the client and senior management.

Those hopes faded at the very first meeting with the client, who'd brought along an expert to inform the team about Millennials as a consumer demographic. This expert presented marketing data and then, to embellish his numerical portrait, provided a detailed list of the Millennial generation's most common characteristics. Millennials, he explained, were overly idealistic, self-involved, impatient to be acknowledged with raises and promotions, and quick to turn their backs if these demands weren't met.

Renée felt powerless to counter his argument. "After hearing all about how Millennials act like we're experts right out of college, and how we all want to be given trophies for our ideas, how could I say anything?" she points out wryly. "It was so uncomfortable."

Yet by far the most eye-opening—and distressing—response came from her colleagues. "I looked around the table, and all the people on my team were nodding their heads in total agreement," Renée recalls. "I remember thinking to myself, 'Is *this* why I'm not getting any development opportunities at this firm? Is this why I'm not advancing?'"

THE NEXT WORKFORCE

Renée's experience illustrates a stubborn paradox in corporate America's treatment of Millennials (the cohort of twenty-one- to thirty-four-year-olds also known as Generation Y). Succession planners and talent specialists recognize that they absolutely need Millennials—who number eighty-three million in the US alone—to step into the leadership gap left by retiring Boomers.[1] It's a gap the far smaller cohort of Gen Xers (who total just 46 million in the US) simply cannot fill.[2] Yet, employers resent having to accommodate Millennials. They're cognizant of the fact that Millennials represent both the future workforce and the most important consumer demographic worldwide, so they court Millennials assiduously, often recruiting promising talent before they even graduate university. Renée, for example, began working for her company as an intern when she was still a college student majoring in psychology. Once

Millennial talent is in the door, however, employers re-sist allocating resources to them.

There is no disputing that Millennials are the next workforce: Millennials represent more than one quarter of the nation's population and 45 percent of the US workforce, outnumbering both Gen Xers and Baby Boomers by a significant margin; by 2025, Millennials will make up 75 percent of the global workforce.[3] Millennials are certainly the most diverse generation to date—44.2 percent of Millennials in the US identify themselves on the Census with an ethnic or racial group other than non-Hispanic white.[4] Many are the children of immigrants, and about 15 percent were born in foreign countries—nearly double the proportion of foreign-born Gen Xers.[5] Young Millennials are also more than three times as likely as adults aged sixty-five and older to identify as LGBT.[6]

Diversity is not the only area where Millennials differ from previous generations. In the US, these men and women have come of age in an era of unprecedented socioeconomic inequality. The wealth gap today is the widest on record: in 2013, the median net worth of the highest income tier of families was almost seven times that of middle-income families and nearly seventy times that of lower-income families.[7] Many Millennials entered the workforce precisely as the global financial system buckled; they were the driving force behind Occupy Wall Street, the sit-in that began in New York City's financial district and swelled into a movement protesting social and economic inequality worldwide.[8] In the wake of the Great Recession, Millennials continue to feel the squeeze of economic uncertainty.[9]

That socioeconomic backdrop helps explain another distinguishing trait of this generation: Millennials are particularly anxious to establish career credentials, as they enter the white-collar workforce more qualified than any previous generation. Sixty-one percent of Millennials in the US have attended college—a talent pool of over fifty million—compared to just 46 percent of Boomers.[10] Ambitious and highly educated, these young employees understandably resent getting coffee and making copies. Indeed, they cannot be perceived as perennial interns, because the imminent exodus of Boomers in leadership leaves a power vacuum that Millennials must fill.

As employers like Renee's clearly grasp, Millennials represent the future of not only the workforce, but also the consumer market, commanding tremendous power both as trendsetters and as customers. In the US alone, Millennial spending power is estimated to reach $200 billion annually by 2017, totaling more than $10 trillion over their lifetimes as consumers.[11] "We look at Millennials as a strategic segment, because they represent such a significant consumer base," agrees Nancy Testa, VP, senior HR business partner, and chief diversity officer at American Express. "They are American Express' current and future Card Members." With Millennials beginning to step into positions of corporate leadership and take control of the purse strings, understanding what motivates this generation will become critical for companies trying to capture not only individual consumers, but also the corporate consumer market.

Millennials are, in short, the bench strength for leadership—and as such, the candidates whom talent specialists and succession planners must prepare, however premature it may seem to do so. But if Renee's story is at all indicative, that's not what companies are doing.

Renée's employer snapped her up as a full-time employee as soon as she graduated, enthusiastic about her passion, skills, and leadership potential. But that initial interest failed to translate, during the eight years of her employment, into investment in her skills growth or leadership development. Training and on-the-job learning never materialized; project management opportunities were offered to older—though not necessarily more experienced—colleagues. The firm's commitment to Renée only worsened after she had her first child and began working from home one day a week. "It's like the hours I put in outside the office don't count," she says, "even though I always deliver, and probably put in more time than my boss." Hence her excitement at the opportunity to show her mettle on the Millennials client team: she thought she was finally getting a chance to stretch her wings.

Renée's experience appears to be typical. Average spending for all corporate training activities (including both employee *and* customer training) amounted to just 0.7 percent of annual revenues in 2013.[12] Part of the reason for this paltry less-than-1-percent investment? Companies are offering on-the-job training to far fewer employees than they used to. In fact, the proportion of employees receiving on-the-job training dropped 42 percent between 1996 and 2008.[13]

Those employees lucky enough to benefit from employer-sponsored training are receiving the bare minimum: in 2014, organizations spent an average of $1,229 per employee on learning opportunities—roughly the same amount they might spend on that employee's annual printing costs.[14] This amounts to a total of just 32.4 hours of training per employee.[15] A paltry 13 percent of that training is dedicated to developing managerial or supervisory skills, a critical area of mastery for a generation poised to step into management roles within the next few years.[16]

Young employees have never been a top priority for companies when it comes to allocating leadership development and training resources. Yet talent management specialists do note that organizations approach Millennials' development differently. "Companies need to find ways to develop talent differently and not in the same ways they did years ago," says Barbara Keen, head of diversity, culture, and organization effectiveness at Novo Nordisk. "In the past, you would ask someone to spend five days getting trained. Today the response is, 'Are you kidding me? I can't take that much time.' We are working hard to make sure our new professionals get the tools they need to be successful in the future. If a company doesn't adjust or doesn't see this as a priority, then future leaders are missing out on an opportunity to grow."

Other talent specialists, particularly those of Generation X, similarly observe that there's been a major culture shift in the way corporations approach young talent. They see a marked difference between their own experience entering the workforce fifteen years ago and that of Millennials entering today. "There's no training, no management development," one HR executive told us. "When I was starting out in the workforce, you knew that they cared about you and that they wanted you to learn. Now, I look around and think, 'Where is the onboarding? Why is no one training these kids?'"

Why, indeed?

THE CASE AGAINST MILLENNIALS

So much research and news coverage have been devoted to the Millennial demographic that it's easy to imagine we know all there is to know about this cohort. In the course of doing this research, we heard talent specialists, business leaders, and Millennials themselves make a host of assertions. Millennials, we were told, have very different priorities than previous generations. Determined to find meaning and purpose in their careers, they are more interested in advancing a global cause than committing themselves to a global corporation. Hungry for recognition, they'd rather build their personal brands than those of their employers. Confident of their worth, or intent on starting up their own companies, they're focused on boosting their own compensation rather than contributing to their companies' bottom lines.

Millennials are thought to be in it for "me me me"—and when companies fail to meet their unrealistic expectations, the story goes, they're out the door in a flash.[17]

Research plays to these themes, reinforcing stereotypes. Jean Twenge's landmark book, *Generation Me*, helped give rise to the notion that Millennials are entitled, narcissistic, and overconfident ("*Generation Me* has never known a world that put duty before self, and believes that the needs of the individual should come first," she writes). The cover of Twenge's book, splashed with an image of a young woman's tattooed midriff adorned with a belly button piercing, rather nicely makes her point that Millennials can't see beyond their own navels.[18] Following the trail that Twenge blazed, an army of publications have succeeded in branding Millennials as the needy "problem children" of the corporate workforce, constantly angling for a trophy, a promotion, or a raise; many of the studies that have attempted to bust these myths have, in effect, only served to reinforce them.[19]

Research diving into subsets of the Millennial cohort hardly bring greater clarity to the portrait. Millennial women, for example, have been the focus of several large-scale studies in recent years—yet the picture painted of young women in the workplace is fuzzy. Are Millennial women finally closing the gender and wage gap? Or are they kicking feminism to the curb and leaning out, rather than in? Consensus is absent among relevant studies.[20] While the very few studies looking at Millennials of color tend to agree that the Millennial generation is far from "post-racial," most research serves to reinforce existing stereotypes: diverse Millennials are seen as highly qualified and tech-savvy employees vested in entrepreneurship, not corporate success.[21] As for economic and micro-generational differences *within* the Millennial generation (such as Millennials from low-income backgrounds, or Millennials over the age of thirty), research is next to nonexistent.

ONE FOOT OUT THE DOOR

The danger of all these stereotypes is that they tend to coalesce, for talent specialists, into one big takeaway: Millennials are a looming flight risk.

In a recent survey of six thousand HR professionals, just one out of every *one hundred* said that Millennials are loyal to their employers.[22] The other ninety-nine fully believe that Millennials are "job hoppers," unwilling to commit to their employers for more than a few years.[23] The global talent head of a multinational consultancy told us that giving Millennials what they want isn't going to make them any more loyal. "*Can* you get these kids to stay?" she challenged. "We cross-train our Millennials, to keep it interesting for them. But we hesitate to send them off to far-flung places for two years, because *they won't stay* with us for two years. We're not going to see the payback. Their next employer will." As another talent specialist clarified, by way of explaining why she wasn't allocating any budget to Millennials' training or development, "Our job is to give back money to our shareholders. We're not a charity."

In short, HR professionals recognize Millennials as their next workforce, but see no reason to groom them for leadership until they start acting, sounding, and looking like previous generations.

That's a mistake with profound implications, as we'll endeavor to show in Part Two. Drawing on two nationally representative surveys—our US survey of 3,298 college-educated men and women working full-time in white-collar professions in the US, and our multimarket survey of 11,936 college-educated men and women working full-time in seven critical markets (Brazil, China, Hong Kong, India, the Philippines, Singapore, and the UK)—in addition to over sixty interviews and several focus groups, we unpack the needs and wants of the Millennial generation. We uncover not only the unparalleled diversity of this generation, but also the tremendous investment opportunity they represent for employers across industry sectors and around the globe.

But first: let's see just how flighty Millennials in the US really are.

2

Who is Flighty?

D o Millennials have one foot out the door? This was an assumption we elected to test. We surveyed 765 college-educated men and women, born between 1982 and 1994, working full-time in white-collar professions in the US. And we indeed uncovered a high incidence of flight risk.

But not among *all* Millennials. We had a hunch that socioeconomics matter—something for which we hadn't tested in our original survey. So we re-fielded to a subset of our original sample. Our hypothesis bore out.

It turns out that, in our nationally representative sample, Millennials who have a financial safety net— those who have families that could support them indefinitely, were they to quit or lose their jobs, or who receive financial gifts from family members totaling at least $5,000 per year—are more likely than those who do not to say they plan to leave their jobs within a year. Fully 40 percent of these financially privileged respondents present, that is, a flight risk. Intuitively, this statistic makes sense: these men and women may be more inclined to explore other options because they can afford to take risks. They have a safety net at the ready should they fail.

But only *9 percent* of Millennials, we find, have such a safety net. The vast majority—91 percent—do not have such financial privilege.

In some ways, this divide should be patently obvious. As noted in Chapter One, the wealth gap is far more pronounced for Millennials than for any prior generation. The US Gini coefficient—a measure of income inequality that shows where a country lies between zero (perfectly equal; everyone's income is the same) and one (perfectly unequal; one individual receives all of the country's income)—has been rising for decades, from 0.362 in 1967 to 0.464 in 2014.[24] Put another way, the wealthy have gotten wealthier while the poor have gotten poorer: household income for the top 1 percent of households grew over *twenty-four times* as much as that of the bottom 20 percent between 1979 and 2007.[25] And those dollars don't stretch as far as they used to. Between 1978 and 2014, the cost of college tuition rose by over 1200 percent—as compared to a roughly 240 percent increase in prices for other consumer goods and services.[26] With national student debt totals hitting $1.2 trillion in 2016, nearly 70 percent of bachelor's degree recipients find themselves saddled with heavy financial burdens before they earn their first paychecks.[27] Little wonder that, in the run-up to the 2016 presidential election, candidates like Bernie Sanders and Donald Trump managed to exceed expectations in winning the votes of Millennials: they tapped into a deep well of frustration among Americans who felt disenfranchised and disempowered by the wealthy and well-established elites in Washington and on Wall Street. [28]

Millennials are, in other words, navigating an economic landscape utterly unlike the one Boomers and Gen Xers faced upon their entry into the workforce—a landscape in which socioeconomic status is as much a deciding factor in career mobility as race and gender are.

The upshot of this uneven financial playing field? The "flighty bunch" stereotype that talent specialists cling to in order to justify stingy budget allocations is grossly misapplied. Failure to take into account socioeconomic realities also explains why so much of the existing research on Millennials serves to amplify the stereotypes. Seen without the filter we applied for financial privilege, Millennials appear not only flighty but downright insatiable in their workplace needs and wants. As we shall see, for the Ninety-One Percent who lack financial privilege, nothing could be further from the truth.

Our research aims to overturn existing false assumptions by answering two critical questions: What do the Ninety-One Percent really need and want from their employers? And why should employers give it to them?

PART TWO: THE OTHER NINETY-ONE PERCENT

3

The Investment Imperative

A s it turns out, Millennials without financial privilege stay at their jobs. Nine out of ten, we find,
have no plans to leave within the next year. Interviews
with some forty-five of these Millennials reveal them
to be committed to their current employers and utterly willing to go the extra mile, investing prodigious
amounts of time and energy in their work in the hopes
that their employers will invest in them in return.

But because talent specialists, as we documented in
Chapter One, tend to see *all* Millennials as a flight risk,
they aren't investing in any of them. We find that only
23 percent of Millennials without financial privilege
have both rewarding relationships and intellectual
growth in their careers—two key factors in determining
employees' abilities to succeed as contributors or leaders
within their organizations.

That does not bode well for the success of those
organizations.

Consider the effects, for example, of withholding
international assignments from Millennials. Since
exposure to other countries, cultures, and consumers

helps give young professionals the knowledge they need to grow those markets and crack open new ones, denying them such exposure or field experience jeopardizes both corporate revenues and future expansion prospects. "Today's globalized and technology-driven economy presents serious challenges," JP Morgan CEO Jamie Dimon points out in a recent *Politico* op-ed. "But it also offers opportunities and rewards skills," he continues, as long as companies make a point of "investing in people [and] training them in the skills employers in their communities are looking for."[29] Stinting on management training likewise imposes a toll, specifically on team productivity and efficiency. Near-term, Millennials will replace Gen Xers as managers, from direct-line supervisors to department heads. If they are ill-prepared for these roles, then upon assuming them they will be consumed by playing catch-up, detracting from their ability to execute on their responsibilities, unlock innovative potential, and deploy talent effectively—to say nothing of the blunders and roadblocks they might encounter along the way.

If leadership development, typically reserved for high-potential talent, is also withheld from Millennials, then the imminent exodus of Boomers (upwards of 50 percent of whom will have exited the workforce by 2020) threatens to pull decades of institutional knowledge and market expertise out the door with them.[30] Typically, talent specialists foment opportunities for cross-generational interaction by inviting high-potential

Millennials to shadow directors, assigning them to work on business-critical projects, and matching them with or exposing them to potential sponsors. Such leadership development initiatives all help to ensure that Millennials acquire not only vital skill sets, but also networks of other up-and-coming leaders, and relationships with executives who will advocate for them. Yet with interaction between these cohorts limited to the occasional reverse mentoring initiative, explicit knowledge transfer—from seasoned executives to future change agents—isn't likely to take place.

As new Millennial hires enter the workforce, well-developed critical-thinking skills are a necessity. Yet, accustomed to crowd-sourced feedback, some Millennials have yet to fully develop these rigorous problem-solving skills—an observation made by Lisa Westlake, CHRO at Moody's and one of several talent specialists to point out this issue. "Millennials seem to solicit a lot of different opinions before moving forward," agrees Novo Nordisk's Barbara Keen. "In some ways, that's one of their greatest strengths. But, the concern is that this could become an overreliance on consensus. As a leader, yes, you do need to be able to make sure that the decisions you make are based on robust data from multiple sources and channels. You also have to be able to synthesize all of that information in context of organizational dynamics, previous investments, and the perspectives of key stakeholders."

Keen acknowledges that critical problem-solving and decision-making skills are a challenge for both new and seasoned leaders. Millennials have an advantage, given their seeming comfort with the vast amount of information at their fingertips, but we have to make it a priority to support their development in these areas. If we don't, she worries about the consequences for the leadership pipeline. "We have to make time for their development. If we don't intentionally help them learn and grow as we have in the past, we are being shortsighted."

LOSING OUT ON DIVERSE LEADERS

Failure to invest in Millennials' career development imperils more than just the leadership pipeline. More critically, because the investment deficit is particularly pronounced for Millennials of color, it undermines the long-term strategic goal of making leadership representative of the workforce and marketplace it serves.

Take Miguel,* for example. During his junior year of college, Miguel was recruited by a major consultancy in the Northeast to be part of its highly competitive internship program. Of Mexican heritage, Miguel was courted by several consultancies, each intent on diversifying not only their slates of high-potential new hires but also their future leadership pipelines. Upon graduation, Miguel accepted the northeastern firm's offer of full-time employment over other offers. He was impressed by the financial investment it had made in recruiting candidates of color, because it seemed to signal commitment to diversifying the top of the house. "My starting cohort was extremely diverse," he says. "I took it as a positive sign that I could have a real career here."

To Miguel's dismay, however, the firm's commitment to diversity began and ended with its recruitment effort. He and his cohort of minority recruits did spend a day at a "strategy college" that introduced them to various types of projects and the skills they would need to become good strategic managers. But over the course of the first year, he says, "our managers simply did not extend a hand to show us the ropes. They seemed to forget that they were once in our same shoes. I'm not saying we needed our hands held, but if a manager would have just shown us how to conduct a client interview, or run a program, that would have been very valuable."

He adds, "If senior leaders were really invested in the future of this company as a diverse organization, you'd think they'd want to do their best to invest in Millennials of color."

We find that a mere 6 percent of black, 9 percent of Hispanic, and 13 percent of Asian Millennials feel they're experiencing rewarding relationships and intellectual growth and challenge at work, as compared to 25 percent of whites. These figures suggest that the diversification of leadership—a project nearly two decades in the making—is an outcome we will not realize anytime soon, despite the fact that as a generation, Millennials are the most diverse to date.[31] The Center for Talent Innovation (CTI) research shows that employees of color are already less likely than their white counterparts to obtain sponsorship, the backing of senior leaders so critical to advancement into the highest echelons of management.[32] An absence of crucial skill development and managerial training can only serve to compound minority talent's invisibility to leaders looking to choose their successors. Given that, as mentioned in Chapter One, close to half of Millennials in the US identify with an ethnic or racial group other than non-Hispanic white, denying this cohort access to growth opportunities and sponsorship is tantamount to ensuring that leadership remains largely white.[33]

BOTTOM-LINE IMPLICATIONS

Failing to capitalize on the inherent diversity of the Millennial generation isn't just a failure for diversity-and-inclusion crusaders. Homogeneous leadership is something companies can ill afford—as a raft of CTI research shows—for two strategic reasons.

First, global growth depends on attracting top talent. And, increasingly, top talent will come from "non-majority" backgrounds. A glance at who has earned tertiary degrees country by country reveals a startling development: 90 percent of the world's white-collar talent pool today is female and/or multicultural.[34] As Miguel explains, this diverse talent tends to favor working for companies that demonstrate not only a commitment to workforce diversity, but also show that talent like themselves can rise to the top. A dearth of diverse role models dooms a global firm to the dregs of the talent pool.

The second reason has to do with innovative potential: our research shows that the firms that are best poised to unlock innovation—and profit from it—are those whose senior leadership is characterized by two-dimensional diversity—that is, leadership that has both inherent diversity (such as age, gender, race, or sexual orientation) and acquired diversity (such as cross-cultural fluency, generational savvy, tech literacy, language skills, or military experience). When leaders both embody difference and embrace it in others, it has a trickle-down effect on corporate culture: at companies where executives have both inherent and acquired diversity, team leaders are 74 percent more likely than leaders at companies lacking this diversity to unlock the innovative potential of team members by fostering a speak-up culture. This boost in innovation has a measureable impact, as such companies are significantly more likely to grow their shares in existing markets and crack open new ones.[35]

To avert the looming crisis in corporate leadership, companies need to see Millennials for the committed cohort they are, and invest in their skill development, innovative potential, and knowledge of other cultures. They also need to foment the relationships critical to their engagement and advancement. In the next two chapters, we'll unpack just what this investment looks like.

4

Intellectual Growth and Challenge

Each year during his undergraduate studies at Brandeis University, Adonis Watkins interned at Lehman Brothers as an analyst, intent on a career in investment banking. With the financial meltdown of 2008, and the collapse of Lehman that same year, Watkins elected to take a detour around Wall Street, accepting an offer at a management consulting firm that advised global investment banks, asset managers, and hedge funds on their technological initiatives.

It seemed a good fit. Most of the personnel had PhDs; many of the senior consultants had been finance executives and portfolio managers. But there was limited investment made in junior talent because, as management explained to Watkins, "You're not driving the revenue." Nor were career growth prospects a given. "People came to work, did their jobs, and went home," says Watkins. "There were no conversations about professional development or career growth opportunities."

In 2012, hungry for development, Watkins accepted an offer to join Moody's Analytics as an analyst. In little more than a year, he moved into a role supporting the sales team as an associate. Today, he's a credit product specialist, managing his own sales region and targets—a goal he'd shared with management when he came on board but whose rapid attainment affirms for him he's found the right company. "During the interview process I was asked about my short and long term career goals. I expressed my interest in pursuing a sales career and was told, 'Perform well in this analyst role, work hard, and build your brand, and we'll provide you with the opportunity to explore that interest,'" he says. "When my managers saw that I could take on a challenging role and perform well, they gave me the opportunity to pursue a sales career at Moody's Analytics. This proved to me that the firm was serious about supporting my career interests and professional development."

What excites him is the sheer range of learning opportunities that lie before him. "It's fairly common, and encouraged, for employees to change roles and explore new challenges within the firm. I have lots of friends who've not only transferred to different departments but also different locations globally including our London, Dubai, and Australia offices." Moody's maintains an intranet site to enable people to apply directly to internal opportunities, and has a mentor program so that, if up-and-comers like Watkins voice their ambitions, senior leader mentors can advocate for, and open doors on behalf of, their mentees. Such relationships between senior leaders and protégés—what CTI defines as sponsorship—provide high-potential talent with the high-octane support and air cover necessary to stretch their boundaries. "I told my mentor that I was interested in going to Asia for an assignment to explore that market and continue my development as a sales professional," Watkins recounts. "That same day, he reached out to the head of sales for the Asia-Pacific region to schedule a call with me to discuss how I could make that a reality. It's a culture that fully supports growth and opportunity."

AN UNMET HUNGER

Watkins's story underscores just how keenly Millennials value opportunities to learn and grow on the job. Fully 73 percent of Millennials without financial privilege say that learning new professional skills is an aspect of intellectual growth that's important to them in their careers. Yet only 55 percent say they have this aspect of intellectual growth in their careers.

Some of this hunger for skill building, our interviewees explain, stems from job insecurity: if you entered the job market after the crash of 2008, you are acutely aware you cannot afford to be perceived as having only one skill set or career path. "Sure, Millennials want flexibility around their roles and chances to learn new things partly because they don't want to get bored," says a thirty-year-old media producer. "My parents and grandparents—they spent twenty years in one role! But it's more about layoffs than boredom for people my age.

We want to develop mastery at a lot of different roles because the job market has changed drastically. We've seen jobs, departments, whole divisions, get phased out. The way I look at my development, you're not going to be able to phase me out if I am proficient in a lot of roles."

As important as building skills, for these young professionals, is achieving expertise and mastery. A robust 69 percent of Millennials without financial privilege identify this as an important aspect of intellectual growth, as well might their employers. But again, for all its importance, employers aren't providing it: an astounding 68 percent of Millennials without financial privilege say they simply aren't realizing this expertise and mastery in their careers.

Neha* used to be one of them. While working for a major US retailer, she was enrolled in a training program with the supposed goal of designing new products for the company. But the "special side projects" she was assigned to develop had no future. "They were just busy work, nothing that would ever become a real product," she says. Worse, the training program mimicked a reality show, where managers piled on more projects to see which trainees would break first. "You couldn't learn from your mistakes: if you made a mistake, you lost a lot of support," she says. "Maybe they thought the reality-TV-show aspect would attract Millennials, but actually it just demoralized us. It was impossible to build more expertise in areas I already had some training in, and I did not feel like I was getting the new skills that would improve my technical or design abilities." Today, Neha is leadership program coordinator at a nonprofit that helps low-income South Asian women and girls expand their horizons. "It's almost a dream job for me," she says. "My manager gave me all the tools I needed and had total faith in me. It's that new economy mentality—give your employees space to expand their horizons, let them have mastery over something, and they will express their initiative."

EAGER TO INNOVATE

Opportunities to innovate also matter to the Ninety-One Percent. More than half of them (56 percent) say that an important aspect of intellectual growth and challenge in their careers is becoming more creative and innovative. That's something employers are acutely intent to harness, as innovation in today's globalized economy is the key to growth. But yet again, our findings point to a glaring gap between what employers acknowledge to be a business imperative and their actual investment in addressing that imperative. Fully 69 percent of Millennials without financial privilege say they don't have this aspect of intellectual growth in their jobs, a finding echoed by many of those we interviewed while they explained why they'd left a previous job for their current employer.

Michele,* an account executive at an up-and-coming advertising agency, left one of advertising's biggest firms out of frustration at being hired for her fresh ideas, only to find that creativity was welcomed only from those working in roles designated as "creative." What appeals to her about her current employer, she says, is that even as an account person, she's empowered to contribute her opinions or solutions at meetings reviewing creative ideas. "There have been a number of situations in which the creative director has taken up an idea I offered," she says, citing a fifteen-second YouTube ad for cough drops that features her innovation.

Yet, even more than seeing her ideas implemented, Michele appreciates the opportunities to expand her skillset to include the creative side of the advertising industry. "I think having that insight into the creative process has helped me a lot in my main role as an account manager," she says. "I can speak the language on the creative side better now. That makes it much easier to communicate our ideas to the client. That would never have happened at my former agency."

INTENT ON UNDERSTANDING PEOPLE UNLIKE THEMSELVES

Another aspect of intellectual growth and challenge that employees—and employers, as noted in Chapter Three—identify as important to their careers is acquiring knowledge of different people and cultures. Many of our interviewees attest to the importance of language skills in bridging divides on their globally dispersed teams. Talent specialists at multinational employers have likewise stressed they won't even consider a candidate who is not willing to be posted internationally. But both qualitative and quantitative evidence points to this aspect of intellectual growth being the least developed: a whopping 73 percent—nearly three out of four—of Millennials without financial privilege say they are not acquiring knowledge of different people and cultures on the job.

One financial services professional lamented that he could not access language training through his employer, even though further expansion of his current responsibilities as an analyst covering Latin America would demand knowledge of Spanish or Portuguese. Another points out that his global employer is so siloed that it's nearly impossible for requests for international assignment from Millennials like himself to be matched up with vacancies from offices abroad. "My employer pays lip service to the geographic preferences that we voice," says this financial services professional, "but there's a fundamental disconnect between requests posted through HR and different parts of the business."

The loss to the business that such underinvestment represents isn't easily quantified, but stories from interviewees like Chris,* a financial analysis manager based in Dubai at a global pharmaceutical company, make clear the extent of the toll. Chris recognized early in his career that in order to have meaningful and sustainable progression, he'd need to have international experience. "Without firsthand exposure to local markets, how can you understand how the price of oil impacts local government or the economy?" he observes. "Terrorism, war, currency devaluation, economic shocks… you may see these topics discussed in a report, but if you didn't experience them you can't manage your business around them." In other ways, too, being in Dubai has given Chris vital insight. "I have much greater appreciation for the difficulties introduced by time zones and cultures. In the Middle East, we work Sunday to Thursday. I am sensitized to religious holidays in a way I might not have been before. Once you live it, you really get it: during Ramadan, for example, people work on a modified work schedule because they're fasting. For thirty days, they're supposed to be working only five to six hours, but they'll be there for eight to ten hours because they are dedicated to their jobs—and they haven't eaten!"

Chris perceives the value of gaining such cultural insights firsthand: "Certainly my experience in Dubai is a big piece of what I will take back when I return to the US and step into a global management role," he says. But he's not at all confident that senior leaders appreciate how important international experience is for global team members, let alone global team leaders. "When I speak to managers back in the States," he says, "most of them aren't looking far enough down the line to see that the future of our company lies outside the US, in Europe, the Middle East, Africa, and Latin America. That's a pretty big oversight, one that's going to cost them a lot more in the long run than what they're reluctant to spend on their people now."

5

Rewarding Professional Relationships

While growing up in New York, Veronica* had always imagined a future for herself in local government. Her parents both worked for the city, and she planned to follow in their footsteps. "Everyone thought I was crazy for limiting myself," she says, recalling her friends' reactions when, upon graduating from Lafayette College in 2007 with a bachelor's degree in sociology and a minor in economics, she made the unpopular decision to apply for a position at the mayor's office. It turned out to be a great move: when the global recession hit in 2008, Veronica held onto her job. She spent the next four years working for various agencies in city government before pursuing a master's degree in urban policy. Upon graduation, she was offered a prestigious internship at a federal agency.

It seemed like a dream come true. "It was one of the most intellectually stimulating environments I'd ever had the opportunity to work in," she remembers. "I was focused on economic policy, an area I'm passionate about. I was on the front lines, getting this insider's view of our legislative system." But something was missing.

"The big problem was that I didn't connect with the people," Veronica explains. The workplace culture was competitive, rather than team-oriented. Coworkers were jockeying for visibility since, as is typical with bureaucracies, the only way to leapfrog the hierarchy was to cultivate a leader's advocacy and protection.

Today, Veronica works for a global financial services firm at which she intends to stay precisely because its culture provides the relationships that she both hungered for and knows will prove critical to her advancement.

"I was very straightforward about what I was looking for," she says, recalling her first interview with the firm. "I wanted to continue working with local governments and policy; I wanted a career where I could grow and advance; and, most importantly, I wanted to be able to build close relationships with senior leaders and coworkers," Veronica explains. And the firm has more than delivered on that promise: Veronica says she can count on her current manager to help her access the development opportunities she needs to grow in her career. "If I want to try something different, to build new skills, I bring my case directly to her," she reflects. "She's in my corner, because she knows I deliver."

WHAT MAKES RELATIONSHIPS MATTER

Few would question Veronica's priorities. Relationships are critical to our satisfaction and engagement at work, and also to our success. We look to coworkers for friendship, but also support in getting our work done. We look to superiors to inspire and motivate us, but also to provide guidance as we navigate the organization. On some level, we realize our journey upward will be that much easier if we can win the backing of someone powerful, someone who believes in our potential and is willing to go out on a limb to help us stretch and grow into positions of leadership.

What we find, however, is that the rewarding professional relationships Millennials seek are in short supply. For example, while a solid 67 percent of Millennials without financial privilege say that inspiration and motivation are important aspects of the rewarding relationships that they want in their careers, only 30 percent say they find that inspiration and motivation in their current workplace relationships. A similar number (64 percent) say they look to their coworkers for support getting their work done—but the majority (65 percent) say they lack this support in their current professional relationships.

Ironically, in an effort to lure and keep Millennial talent, companies accommodate or even insist on furnishing Millennials with remote working arrangements—denying Millennials the exposure they need to cultivate key relationships. "The objective should be to find the right balance between flexibility and physical presence," observes Moody's Lisa Westlake. "If a Millennial is accustomed to a flexible work arrangement where they often work out of the office, it may be harder to gain the exposure to senior leaders needed for advancement."

For example, Westlake recalls discussing flexible work arrangements with a team leader who manages software developers. He was reticent to allow the team to work remotely since they would have their morning scrum early each day to discuss the issues they needed to resolve. According to Westlake, the leader felt the team was more productive when everybody was physically present, which is notable given this is an IT team who could essentially do their jobs from anywhere.

Westlake has also observed that the socially-connected-every-minute Millennial generation must become better at building the kind of "offline" relationships they need and crave at work. "They're great at joining a LinkedIn group, but that isn't helping them develop their interpersonal skills. Our most effective leaders are adept at building and leveraging in-person relationships to drive results and are recognized for their ability to communicate effectively with others through various channels."

The experience of Deb,* a Millennial account coordinator for a public relations firm in LA, underscores the bottom-line impact of underdeveloped work relationships. She left her previous job because of inefficiencies resulting from a near-total lack of contact among colleagues. "There were maybe one or two people in my department whom I could trust to handle my projects with no oversight," she says. "But if I had to give a task to someone in programming, for example, when it came back it was always on me to check that person's work and redo it if necessary—and it often *was* necessary." In contrast, relationships with her team at her current employer ensure she has plenty of time to develop her leadership skills. "I'm lucky to have a great relationship with my team now," Deb says of her co-workers at her current employer. "I trust them to double- and triple-check their own work, so I don't have to waste time micromanaging."

Millennials grasp this: fully 64 percent of our Ninety-One Percent group acknowledge the importance of relationships that allow colleagues to learn from those with expertise they lack. But the majority (53 percent) do not have them. Hector,* a junior brand manager in the pharmaceutical industry, offers some insight as to why. When Hector first joined his company, he made a concerted effort to reach out to more experienced colleagues and managers in order to gain the expertise he saw he needed to get ahead. But his efforts rarely paid off. Managers were standoffish, he says, inclined to give his cohort lists of assignments, but not inclined to build relationships with them. "We younger guys just don't hold their interest," he says. "They're not eager to be our mentors, and they're not interested in whether or not we're prepared to take the next steps in our careers. They're more focused on their own advancement."

The saving grace for Hector has turned out to be his career counselor, a woman who's taken an interest in his growth and sets up regular meetings over coffee to see how he's doing—a rarity among managers, as far as he can see. "Managers are usually just a face with a name," he says. "They're there, but they never really interact with you." His counselor, in contrast, pings him regularly on instant messenger to see how things are going on a new project he's started; she even contacted people already on the project to insist they reach out to him and show him the ropes. "You learn so much more from the people around you when you build ties with them," Hector observes.

THE RELATIONSHIP MILLENNIALS NEED TO GET RIGHT

Alexandra Hille, an account coordinator at News America Marketing, can pinpoint why she's confident she made the right choice in recently joining the firm: she's forged a rewarding relationship with the SVP of her department, whom she sees and interacts with daily, despite the chasm in their titles and experience. "I've started doing projects for her, even though she's my boss's boss, because even though I'm young and haven't been there that long, she trusts me to do things for her and her clients," Hille observes. "Just knowing that someone at that level would take an interest in my career, would treat me like a friend and give me sound advice—that's huge, in terms of my future here."

What Hille is describing is sponsorship: the relationship a young professional forges with a leader who believes in him or her and is willing to put his or her name forward behind closed doors, to push for his or her promotion, and to create projects or roles to grow the protégé's skills and showcase them to top executives. Research that CTI has conducted on sponsorship affirms what Millennials seem innately to understand: with sponsors, employees are much more likely to ask for raises, to feel satisfied with their rates of advancement, and to hang onto their ambition as they rise through the ranks.[36] The sponsor effect, as we call it, is measurable: women with sponsors are 19 percent more likely to be satisfied with their rates of advancement than women without sponsors; people of color with sponsors are 56 percent more likely.[37]

A sponsor is not someone that management is obliged to furnish to rising stars. Sponsorship must be earned in many of the ways Hille embodies; by giving 110 percent, being willing and at-the-ready for assignments beyond those in the job description, and demonstrating enormous potential, she won the attention and garnered the support of her boss's boss, a woman who, in turn, inspires and motivates Hille to raise her game and up her commitment to the organization.

What made that relationship possible, however, are a culture and physical environment that downplay hierarchical distances. The hierarchy is there; Hille has enormous respect for what separates her from her sponsor in terms of field experience, subject expertise, and institutional knowledge. But sponsorship finds a ready seedbed in the proximity of seasoned professionals to Millennials eager to prove themselves. "She doesn't talk down to me," Hille explains. "There's a culture of teamwork that helps put us on even footing. We get along on a personal level, too. She's really into fitness: she gets up at three-forty-five a.m. to go to the gym, which takes such motivation and dedication, and she clearly applies that to her career as well. She's an inspiration."

The environment Hille describes at her previous employer, in contrast, wasn't one in which sponsorship was ever likely to occur between herself and her superiors. She worked for a corporate recruiting firm where, within two months, she'd established herself as a star producer, making two placements in half the time it took even seasoned colleagues to make one. The money was good; bonuses were generous. "I realized I could be earning six figures by the time I was twenty-four," says Hille. But she left after three months because the culture was never likely to yield the relationships she craved. No one stood out as a role model. No one was interested in helping her advance. On the contrary, she felt bullied by her senior colleagues, who resented her for showing them up. "The whole culture was very military-esque," she says. "They thought by punishing you, by knocking down your self-esteem, you'd be inspired to do better. I didn't feel 'lucky to be there.' I felt beaten down."

Given the smaller size of Generation X, building sponsor relationships between Millennials and Boomers is critical to ensuring a robust pipeline of future leaders—yet our data shows that Hille's experience at her previous employer is far from the exception. While 59 percent of Millennials without financial privilege recognize, like Hille, the importance of people who might help them advance in their careers, only 29 percent say they have such people in their work lives. Even fewer Millennials have the backing of a senior leader whom they could call a sponsor: just 5 percent of Millennials at large companies (those with over fifty thousand employees) overall have a sponsor according to CTI's definition.[38]

LESS LIKELY TO GET THE RIGHT RELATIONSHIPS: MINORITIES

Sponsorship can be particularly scarce for Millennials of color, like Petra.* Aiming for a career as a public defense attorney, Petra landed a position as a legal assistant at a state adoption law firm after college. She spent the next two years working her way up to paralegal, while simultaneously studying for the LSATs. The office was very small, very old-school, very male, and very pale. "All the lawyers were white," says Petra, who is of Filipino heritage. "I didn't expect it to bother me—I grew up in Seattle, not exactly the most diverse city— but I quickly realized that the lawyers favored white paralegals over me, even when I was doing superior work." Cases that she was far more qualified to handle found their way into the hands of her colleagues. Over time, the lawyers came to trust, and advocate for, those who most reminded them of themselves. "It wasn't conscious on their part," Petra reflects. "I don't think they realized what they were doing."

Our research supports Petra's observations: in our 2012 report, *Vaulting the Color Bar*, we found that employees of color are less likely to be sponsored than their white peers. Part of that dearth of sponsorship can be attributed to unconscious bias: leaders are more likely to take on protégés with whom they share common cultural and ethnic ground, as it's simply easier to build trust with people like oneself.[39] This unconscious tendency is compounded by the fact that many executives of color, eager to avoid accusations of favoritism in the wake of affirmative action hiring measures, often *consciously* hesitate to sponsor minority employees.

Yet sponsorship, we demonstrate, is *the* critical career lever for minority talent: 53 percent of African Americans who have sponsors are satisfied with their rates of advancement, compared with 35 percent of those who lack sponsors; 55 percent of Asians who have sponsors are satisfied with their rates of advancement, compared with 30 percent of those who lack sponsors; 61 percent of Hispanics who have sponsors are satisfied with their rates of advancement, compared with 43 percent of those who lack sponsors.[40]

At firms like Petra's, the scarcity of sponsors for Millennials compounded by the scarcity of sponsors for people of color sends a signal that is particularly discouraging for high-potential Millennials of color who dream of achieving top positions. Lacking the sponsorship she needed to advance, Petra certainly couldn't see herself achieving a position of leadership within her firm. "When I tried to look ahead, I couldn't see any opportunities there for me. I kept my job, because I needed to pay my bills, but I was just treading water."

A CASE STUDY IN CONFLICT RESOLUTION

Two years ago, Novo Nordisk recruited a sales force of roughly three hundred high achievers new to the pharmaceutical industry with the goal of maximizing sales among a unique set of healthcare providers. About one hundred of the new reps, which included a heavy Millennial presence, emerged as stellar performers and drove revenues that no one had expected. So the company took a bold step, merging them into the broader organizational sales force.

Not every division director welcomed the newcomers. To many of the Gen Xers in charge, the younger reps had irregular work habits, unorthodox methods, and an insatiable need for recognition. "Friction was high," says Andy Ajello, senior vice president in national diabetes and obesity sales, "especially around the perception that Millennials need constant feedback." Boomers, in turn, complained that the younger reps' tendency to text and email them instead of calling or arranging meetings bordered on insubordination. "They basically wanted reps to communicate up the same way they did," observes Ajello.

However, hoping to roll out five new medicines in the next five years, Ajello realized that leaders couldn't afford to turn their backs on younger members of the new sales force. "If we don't make an attempt to listen to them, or if we insist we're not going to communicate by email and text, then we're going to miss out on some great ideas," he says, citing an Instagram campaign that sparked interest in Novo Nordisk's diabetes therapies with photos of the sales reps' bicycle team in Copenhagen.

So Ajello organized a workshop. He brought in his leadership team and, with the help of some noted experts and some Millennials, elicited questions, brokered alliances, and helped each generation emerge with a better appreciation for each other's strengths. It proved so successful, he replicated the experience in Miami, pulling in the broader leadership team of thirty-three regional business directors. "They get it!" he says. "They get that Millennials are our future workforce, and that we need to invest in them just as we do the rest of our workforce. The directors who are putting in the time to teach their more junior reps, inspire them, coach them—they're seeing phenomenal results. The more junior sales force members have become more engaged."

The biggest shift is still in the works: Ajello wants to put line managers through the training, as whatever loyalty a director cultivates can be readily undermined by a manager who refuses to acknowledge the reps' extra work. Ajello recognizes that with ten reps each to oversee, managers often struggle to provide the developmental feedback and career coaching that each rep needs and expects. "They just aren't set up to provide mentoring along with their other responsibilities, so some of our top performers have left," says Ajello. But he's confident that the new training will better equip managers to provide professional development to their staff and help Novo Nordisk retain its innovative sales force.

6

What the Ninety-One Percent
Actually Values

What's misunderstood about Millennials, we've endeavored to show, is their loyalty: once you filter for financial privilege, it becomes clear that the vast majority of this talent cohort intends to stick around and give their employers everything they've got.

If other stereotypes—that Millennials yearn for meaning and purpose; for recognition; and for higher compensation—endure, it's because they do in fact get at important truths about this generation. We find, for example, that 72 percent of Millennials without financial privilege rate meaning and purpose as very important in their careers. Fully 65 percent prioritize high compensation, and 45 percent say that recognition is very important in their careers.

But what's critical to understand is how Millennials without financial privilege define these values. Our survey reveals nuances to what Millennials identify as priorities—nuances that cast these young men and women in a whole new light.

MEANING AND PURPOSE

Perception: "Millennials want to advance a global cause."
Reality: "I want to achieve the goals set before me."

For Millennials without financial privilege, finding meaning and purpose at work is pretty straightforward. Most are not looking to jump ship for the nonprofit world or kick-start their own ventures: only one in three (33 percent) say advancing causes they care about is an important aspect of meaning and purpose in their careers. For 71 percent, what is important is achieving the goals set before them.

Sara Weil, a global diversity and inclusion manager at the Moody's New York office, is a case in point. In her previous role in procurement, Weil recalls working on a particularly tough project with a senior executive in IT. The executive, who was not familiar with procurement procedure, reached out to the vendor himself to negotiate pricing. By the time he looped Weil in on the agreement, she saw that there was a significant opportunity to get a better deal. "I explained to him that I have creative ways of negotiating with this vendor when I communicate with them directly, and I gave my reasoning," Weil recalls. The executive agreed with her rationale, but Weil sensed that her words would have a bigger impact if she could demonstrate her negotiating skills in real time—by contacting the vendor herself and getting the executive more than he thought possible. "So I made it my goal to do just that." Weil says. "When the deal went through, the executive was impressed—he sent an email to my manager, my managing director, and the CIO essentially saying, 'I didn't follow the process, but Sara managed to negotiate an even better deal when I already knew we were under their internal margin limits.'"

Getting kudos from a senior leader was certainly gratifying, Weil agrees, but the success of the procurement deal itself was more motivating. "At the end of the day, I get satisfaction from knowing that I helped Moody's get the best services at the best rate," she observes. Meaning and purpose on the job, according to Weil, comes down to the boost she gets from excelling in a new responsibility, achieving a career goal—such as successfully making a lateral move into the D&I space where she now works—or exceeding expectations on a project. "That's what I go to work for—that sense of accomplishment is really meaningful."

Companies that help Millennials accomplish their goals reap noticeable benefits. To hear Niki Patel tell it, Novo Nordisk is one of them. Patel is a medical liaison, working in a clinical capacity with thought leaders—a job she secured after completing a fellowship program with the organization. She has a Doctorate of Pharmacy degree (PharmD), and is currently working on her MBA. "I'm always striving to learn more, and hope to become a leader in an organization driving strategies to improve outcomes for patients," she explains.

She's well on her way. Despite being one of the youngest people on her national team, her work has already been recognized at the executive level. Patel was named Rookie of the Year for her first year performance, in part because of her passion and drive to understand and meet customer needs. She was the sole person on her team to submit a solution in Novo Nordisk's crowdsourcing Idea Stream contest—it placed among the top ten of forty submissions. She is recognized as a powerful collaborator and driving force for her team on various internal projects and she also won one of five prizes awarded to outside-the-box thinkers for Novo Nordisk's Take Action Challenge for her proposal to involve employees company-wide in a national children's charitable health initiative.

Patel contrasts the responsiveness of management at Novo Nordisk with the recalcitrance of management at her former employer, prior to getting her PharmD. "I've always had lots of creativity, energy, and passion to get things done and try new things," she says, "but when I tried to do that in a previous role, I got squashed." She adds, "This was my first professional job, so having an encouraging mentor to help me reach my career goals was something I really wanted."

Committed to making an impact in health education, Patel is thrilled to finally be in a place where her passion and energy are supported and channeled towards meaningful goals. "Having these initiatives such as the Idea Stream Project and Take Action Challenge to support me in making an impact in the world we live in makes me proud to work for Novo Nordisk," she says.

"I'm proud to work somewhere that shares my value for the community. It keeps me engaged. Honestly, right now I can't see my future anywhere else."

HIGH COMPENSATION

Perception: "Millennials want higher pay to support a lifestyle they haven't yet earned."
Reality: "I want to know that I will to be able to support myself moving forward."

Millennials have a bad reputation when it comes to money. Employers and economists alike shake their heads at Millennials' alleged propensity to spend on international travel rather than home ownership, their inclination to invest in risky entrepreneurial ventures rather than in savings or retirement accounts, and their YOLO-inflected ("You Only Live Once") tendency to "rent" a lifestyle beyond their means—evidence, they believe, of Millennials' impulsive and immature approach to financial stewardship.[41]

For the Ninety-One Percent, this picture couldn't be further from the truth. The vast majority (82 percent) say that an important aspect of high compensation is the financial security it affords them.

Given that financial security is something many Millennials have sorely lacked for much of their lives, this finding shouldn't come as a surprise. The Millennial generation has weathered protracted economic and social uncertainty on a scale unknown to their parents. Those born in the early- to mid-1980s entered adult-

hood just as the dotcom bubble burst and terrorists took
down the World Trade Center. In the wake of those cat-
aclysms, the 2007 mortgage crisis plunged the nation
and the globe into recession. Millennials witnessed
family and friends lose homes, jobs, and lifetime savings—and many saw their own economic opportunities
shrink.[42] They may be the first generation that does not
surpass their parents in wealth, property ownership,
and social mobility. The reality of wage stagnation and
sluggish global growth means that they are working
more and saving less—the projected retirement age
for Millennials is over seventy-three, compared to six-
ty-two for Boomers—and most expect to retire without
the benefit of meaningful social security payments.[43]

Exacerbating this gloomy economic forecast is
the rising cost of college tuition: outstanding student
debt in the US totaled more than $1.2 trillion in
2014, with the average college graduate owing almost
$30,000 in student loans.[44] Many owe far more: one
interviewee admitted that the $120,000 he owes will
have a significant impact on his career decisions for the
foreseeable future. He graduated college with $40,000
in outstanding loan obligations, but after working
for several years in the healthcare industry, realized
he would need another degree to fulfill his dream
of managing a community hospital. Enrolling in a
master's of health administration program has added
another $80,000 to his debt burden. "I'm not putting
much into savings, because I have to pay off the interest

on my loans," he explains. "Impressing my friends is the furthest thing from my mind."

A mere 15 percent of Millennials say impressing others is an aspect of high compensation that they value, and only 35 percent say that having greater latitude in their career choices—having the option, say, of leaving their job to start up a company—is important. Far more important, our interviews reveal, is paying off student loans; managing rent, utilities, or other cost-of-living expenses; and ensuring future financial stability.

Other interviewees reveal that they have financial responsibilities to their families or communities, particularly those born outside the US. Ibi Krukrubo is one of them: an audit partner today, he recalls a moment in his career when he considered leaving EY for a number of reasons, including an offer from another employer to make more money. It was an enticing offer, particularly for someone who has provided some level of support for members of his extended family since he started with EY at age twenty-one. Still, Krukrubo eventually turned down the offer, conscious that EY was investing in his leadership potential and career in ways that went beyond salary.

"It's not about making enough money to be on the cover of *Forbes*," says Krukrubo of his decision to stay at EY. "I certainly want to be compensated enough to take care of my family, and ultimately be financially secure, but for me personally, the money in itself is not a factor. It is really about the combination of experiences and impact I can have being at the firm that is hard to duplicate anywhere else." Other interviewees echo Krukrubo's sentiments: compensation, these Millennials explain, needs to be high enough to provide for themselves and for their loved ones; but beyond that, compensation simply isn't enough of a motivator to draw Millennials away from a company that offers opportunities to learn new skills, build rewarding relationships, and progress in their careers.

"I've been at EY for most of my adult life," Krukrubo observes. "In that time, I've grown up as a professional and as an individual. I owe a lot of who I am as a person to my time here, the relationships I've built, and the values that we hold as an organization. That's more valuable to me than a paycheck."

RECOGNITION

Perception: "Millennials want a trophy so they can build their personal brand outside work."
Reality: "I want my loved ones to understand and approve of my career."

If there is one stereotype that talent specialists are loath to abandon, it is that Millennials simply cannot get through a day without someone affirming their worth.

"A big challenge for some Millennials," says Moody's Lisa Westlake, "is the expectation of continuous feedback. They seem to want constant assurance they're valued and that the work they are doing is valuable. That's somewhat different from previous generations, where you gained experience and knowledge by delivering results first, and then the feedback and benefits followed. It's not a work-ethic problem, just a difference in understanding of how performance leads to advancement."

Diana Cruz Solash, EY Americas Ethnicity Leader, agrees that recognition is highly important to Millennials, more than to previous generations. "But it's more because they want to understand how they contribute to the business strategy," she clarifies. Millennials want to be recognized for the value they provide and want leaders to seek out their opinions. At EY, partners and executives are expected to help all associates see their impact. "As with everything else, Millennials want 'just-in-time' feedback, so we give it to them right away," Cruz Solash says. EY has also stepped up efforts to reward employees with recognition: "Applause Awards" can be sent by anyone, to anyone—with copies sent to the recipient's manager. Likewise, EY has a central online feedback system to enable employees to recognize managers for on-the-job (OTJ) coaching. If a manager gets recognized, he or she will receive a note from the system saying, "You've been recognized for providing OTJ coaching," with verbatim comments on the impact the manager had on the person, or persons, they coached and motivated.

But whether companies embrace the need for recognition or seek to correct for it, it's not likely to go away. The story that Shaun,* a cable sports network producer, told us helps explain why.

When Shaun graduated college, journalism degree in hand, his parents expressed concern at his intent to pursue a job in sports broadcasting. "I think they had pictured something like law or medicine for me," says Shaun, who is African American and the first in his family to earn a college degree. Both of his parents had begun working right out of high school and remained in their jobs ever since. So when he shared with them the letter he received from a major sports news network offering him employment, their first response was one of disappointment. "My dad looked at the salary stated in the letter," Shaun recalls, "and said, 'Well, where's the rest of it?' He and my mother were shocked at how low my compensation was, starting out in media."

Shaun took the job anyway; seven years later, he is an associate producer, overseeing everything from producing sit-down interviews between athletes and celebrities to generating fresh segment ideas. He's also the primary producer for a weekly pre-game segment.

Still, he wishes to show his parents just how well he is doing. "I'm successful, but success in media isn't so easy to explain, especially when you're behind the scenes," he says. "I'm not a newscaster, I'm not front and center in any of the shows. My compensation has gone up with my promotions, yes, but it's nowhere near what I could be making in finance or law."

For more than two out of three Millennials without financial privilege (68 percent), making their families proud is an important aspect of the recognition they want in their careers. Yet many of our interviewees find it a challenge, because jobs like cybersecurity analyst, healthcare navigator, and social media strategist simply didn't exist a generation ago.[45] "When your work is measured in Facebook likes," as one Millennial explains, "it can be hard to show others you're successful."

In Shaun's case, recognition was one way to show his parents how much he appreciates the sacrifices they made for him. "They worked long hours for the paycheck," he says, "so that I could have the opportunity to do something I love. I want them to know how thankful I am for their hard work—and that I've made something of myself as a result." So it was particularly gratifying to Shaun when *Vibe* magazine named him in an article about one of the network's shows. "We took a risk and collaborated with a famous producer to revamp the opening theme, and it went over extremely well," he says. His boss, impressed, made sure that collaboration was attributed to Shaun when *Vibe* interviewed her for the article. "She didn't even tell me!" Shaun exclaims. "I didn't find out I was named until I read the story in *Vibe.*" He immediately sent the article to his parents. "Of course getting my name out there is nice, but more importantly my parents have stopped worrying about me," he says. "Now they have tangible proof that I'm doing well."

Often, Millennials without financial privilege belie the assumption that Millennial employees are just gunning for a trophy, accustomed to being rewarded with one whether they beat out the competition or simply show up. They're not looking for fame: only 14 percent say that making themselves known in the world is an important aspect of recognition.

Instead, the Ninety-One Percent view recognition in a much more communal way than the "me me me" stereotype would suggest. "When I think about being recognized for success, the focus for me is my team and my family," notes Justin Angelle, a Louisiana district business manager at Novo Nordisk and father of four. "Respect and recognition from my coworkers are the best rewards—next to getting those things from my kids, of course!" Another Millennial parent explained that, to her, recognition means working hard in her career to become a role model for her young daughter. "My husband and I want to raise our daughter to believe she can do anything. I realized that the most important thing I could do for her is excel in my career. I want to show her what success can look like, so she grows up with that source of empowerment." Or, as Shaun sums up, "Recognition symbolizes that your hard work is being seen by the people who matter most."

ANSWERING THE MILLENNIAL CALL

So yes, Millennials want things: to achieve their goals, to be compensated fairly, and to be recognized by the people who matter to them. What a few employers are only just beginning to understand? Companies could do far worse than give Millennials want they want—and need.

"The perception that we need to turn the workplace on its head to satisfy Millennials just isn't accurate," observes Nancy Testa, chief diversity officer at American Express. "Millennials are looking for career growth, competitive pay, and purposeful careers—things every generation wants. It's the delivery that's changing, and frankly, it's changing in a way that improves the workplace for everyone." EY's Diana Cruz Solash agrees. "We find that Millennials get blamed for wanting or needing things like flexibility or feedback. But guess what? The world won't fall apart if we deliver. In the end, the way we're changing our approach to learning, flex time, and recognition will benefit our entire workforce."

SPOTLIGHT ON BRAZIL

Brazilian Millennials—or Gen Ys as they are more commonly known in Brazil—are said to act like they have the world at their feet. They want salary increases and quick promotions; they want more senior responsibilities without "paying their dues"; they want social media access in the office; and they want the option to work from home. With their ever-growing list of demands, Brazilian Millennials seem to their employers to be impossible to satisfy.[46]

In some ways, the findings of our global multimarket survey support these stereotypes: 86 percent of Millennials in Brazil *do* value recognition at work, and 81 percent say that high compensation is very important as well. Indeed, a stunning 28 percent of Brazilian Millennials say they intend to leave their employers within the year.

That's not necessarily a bad thing, says thirty-one-year-old Gina,* a market analyst currently working for an international bank in São Paulo. "My parents couldn't afford to change jobs when they were my age, even if they had to work eighteen-hour days and never received a promotion or a bump in pay," she says. "The way they worked was exploitative."

Beating Back the Specter of Instability

Brazil has changed a lot in the past several decades. Its military dictatorship ended in 1985, with the current constitution enacted in 1988.[47] This makes Millennial-age Brazilians the first in decades to grow up free from the political repression and economic stagnation that characterized previous generations' working lives. "When I was young, the inflation was incredible," one Gen Xer remembers. "If you went to the supermarket in the morning, you would try to buy as much as you could, because prices would be higher in the afternoon!" Currency fluctuation was so common that savings might have been completely lost overnight, another interviewee explains. "My parents had to start from scratch multiple times."

The institution of the Plano Real in 1994 tempered inflation and stabilized the economy, and economic expansion exploded in the early 2000s.[48] Gina, who came of age during this economic boom, doesn't feel the level of financial anxiety that kept her parents tied to their less-than-ideal jobs. "I don't have to accept those bad working conditions," she says. "There's more opportunity and more mobility, so Gen Ys can stand up for themselves and expect more out of their careers."

But the shifting nature of the Brazilian workforce—Brazil has the seventh-highest rate of employee turnover in the world—is something that companies have been slow to accommodate.[49] As Claudio,* a Millennial and senior-level account manager at an advertising agency in Rio de Janeiro, comments, "There's next to no onboarding and promotions are slow because companies are not used to accommodating people who change jobs or have diversified skill sets. It's a serious issue, not just for Millennials, but for older employees, too."

In 2015, Brazil's economy took a dramatic downturn: the rate of unemployment among Brazilian Millennials hovered just below 16 percent during 2015, and underemployment poses an even larger problem.[50] The recession has hit Millennials much harder than older generations because, as the last to arrive, they are the first to be cut. Those coming right out of college see job-hopping as a necessity. "My dad was able to settle down at one company and work there for forty years," says Luiza,* a recent graduate. "Right now, it's much harder to manage that permanence because of the financial crisis." Even those Millennials who actively choose to leave their jobs may not be doing so entirely due to their own wishes. "If they sense they're about to be fired, some Gen Ys would rather quit first," Luiza explains. "They're worried that it will be a stain on their resumes otherwise. Companies prefer they leave, too, so they encourage it."

The Generation Gap

Technology usage—particularly social media—is another source of generational friction in the Brazilian workplace. Brazilian Millennials are among the most optimistic about technology: 65 percent believe that communicating virtually with their team helps them save time on the job, and 46 percent say that it enhances productivity. The average Brazilian Millennial has seven social media profiles, with Facebook and Instagram being among the most popular platforms.[51] "There's a joke that Gen Y's can't even go to the toilet without their cell phones," says one Millennial-age employee. "I have an older colleague who will actually check to see if we've taken our cell phones when we leave for lunch or go to the toilet!"

Despite their comfort with social media and virtual communication, Brazilian Millennials seem to feel that key workplace interactions should happen in person.

We find among those we surveyed a preference for in-person interaction in conducting initial meetings with colleagues and clients, brainstorming sessions, providing feedback (both positive and negative), and sharing difficult company news. As our interviewees clarify, virtual technology *supplements* in-person communication; it doesn't replace it. "Technology helps with work productivity in certain ways, but when it comes to workplace relationships it feels too robotic to me," explains a Millennial working in media. "Even though I work in a very tech-heavy environment, I don't think it can take the place of in-person contact."

That lack of face time may be a factor in Brazilian Millennials' high flight risk: 27 percent of those who plan to leave their current jobs within a year cite a lack of visibility with power players at their companies as the reason they plan to leave their current positions. Moreover, for 23 percent of Millennials, lack of face time with senior leaders is a barrier to forming relationships with leaders who have the potential to advance their careers. "It's a trap that I feel companies are falling into," Luiza agrees. "Companies think that the way to attract and retain Gen Ys is to put everything on social media platforms, when building solid professional relationships really requires in-person contact."

Brazilian Millennials certainly grasp that solid relationships will be the career lever that fulfills their aspirations for top jobs. Aline Santos, office manager at S&P Global in São Paulo, says that traveling to build connections with her far-flung team—which covers Argentina and Brazil—has been key to her success. "I've made it a point to meet with everyone on my team, and to make myself available to share ideas and communicate," she says. "As a Gen Y myself, I know I appreciate that face-to-face contact. Since the beginning of my career, I have always believed that we need to be the kinds of managers that we would like to have."

SPOTLIGHT ON THE UK

Quality of life is the top priority for Millennial employees in the UK, as 76 percent of the UK Millennials we surveyed in our global multimarket survey affirm. Of the 22 percent of Millennial Brits in our survey who plan to leave their jobs within the next year, 18 percent say expectations of 24/7 availability is a factor in their decision to leave, and 17 percent say that lack of respect for their personal time is pushing them out the door. At first glance, these statistics appear to confirm the media's worst stereotypes—and employers' worst nightmares—about the lazy, self-involved, and entitled youth.[52] But dig just a little deeper, and the truth is revealed to be far more nuanced.

For one thing, many Millennials' reasons for wanting work-life balance are hardly self-involved. "There's this perception that Millennials have no responsibilities outside of work, that we're all just hanging out at the pub or watching telly after hours, but that's not true," says twenty-six-year-old Clara,* a single mother who works full-time for a film distribution company. "After work, I go pick up my toddler from day care. I make her dinner, give her a bath, put her to bed—and then I often get on my computer and work for another three hours." From childcare and mortgage payments to supporting younger siblings or aging parents, the majority of the Millennials we interviewed shoulder significant responsibilities in addition to the demands of their careers. This is particularly true of foreign-born and first-generation individuals—two of the fastest-growing demographics in the UK.[53] "My parents lost most of their savings in the 2008 downturn," one foreign-born Millennial told us. "So whatever is left of my paycheck after covering my own living expenses, I send that to them."

Out of Sight, Out of Mind

Troublingly, many UK Millennials feel that honoring these familial commitments compromises their chances at professional success. As a recent YouGov poll revealed, one in three workers polled believe their employers consider those prepared to put work before family as more productive; among Millennials, that proportion rises to two fifths.[54] Clara sometimes wonders if her choice to work from home in the evenings so she can take care of her daughter has stunted her career. "I do think it's held me back. From a manager's perspective, one employee leaves at 1700 on the dot, while this other employee always stays until 1900 or 2000. It doesn't matter that I work late every day at home, because he doesn't *see* me putting in those hours."

Clara is far from alone in her struggle to remain professionally visible while working from home. While some companies have begun to adopt policies that reflect a desire to be sensitive to employees' obligations outside the office, such as flex time and virtual working arrangements, according to the Millennials in our survey, virtual work arrangements—often considered a panacea for work-life balance issues—don't improve their quality of life: just 9 percent feel that virtual methods of communicating with their teams give them work-life balance. So what is the missing ingredient that makes working remotely feasible? The Millennials we interviewed have an answer: trust.

"Since I started in sales, my manager has always made it clear that specifically when and where I complete my work matters less than doing high quality work and meeting my deadlines," explains Sarah Goodwin, launch brand manager at Baxalta. Goodwin believes that having a trusting relationship with her manager is the key to making a remote working arrangement productive—for both herself and the company. "That kind of work arrangement only works for us because my manager doesn't feel the need to monitor me doing my work—he trusts me to get things done on my schedule," she says. Goodwin has certainly delivered on that trust: in 2014 alone, she brought in £15 million worth of business for the UK sales team. "I don't think I could have been so successful in an environment where I was being constantly micromanaged," she reflects. We heard her observations affirmed by other young Brits. "Having the ability to work from home is great, but it means even more that my employer just acknowledges that there are sometimes other demands on my time," one agreed. "Having a boss I can go to and say, 'Look, my mom is sick, I need to take her to the doctor,' and that boss then trusting me to get my work done—that's what makes a difference."

Economic Burdens

It's not just family obligations, however, that weigh heavily on British Millennials' minds and careers. With post-recession incomes failing to keep pace with rising student debt and cost of living, savings are increasingly becoming a luxury that many Millennials simply can't afford; as a result, Millennials in the UK will have to put off retirement far longer than previous generations.[55] The 2008 recession also left a deep impression on the Millennial generation, shaking their faith in the traditional pension schemes their parents bought into. "It's hard to save enough for a real pension, because cost of living is very high, so that's part of it," agrees one business analyst at a London financial firm. "But the recession also changed the way a lot of Millennials think about saving. I saw the older generation work hard and invest their savings in all the right places, but their pensions still went up in smoke. Having seen that,

I want good quality of life now, while I'm working—because by the time I'm sixty-five, I may not be able to retire."

Given that Millennials are starting their careers with the expectation of a lifelong commitment, it comes as no surprise that many want more out of their jobs than a nine-to-five slog. "My career is a huge part of my identity," explains Tamar,* a human resources officer for a consulting firm in London. "I know that I will never give up work, not just for financial reasons, but because I get a sense of worth and purpose out of it." Our findings mirror Tamar's investment in her career. Like Tamar, 72 percent of Millennials surveyed in the UK want meaning and purpose in their careers; the same percentage want intellectual growth. As one Millennial who has been working for his employer for over nine years explained, "I don't have a particular job spec. My work varies broadly day to day, which keeps me learning and keeps me engaged. I don't think I would have stayed so long if that weren't the case."

Addressing Millennials' desire for meaning and intellectual growth on the job doesn't require a major corporate overhaul. As this Millennial remarks, "Companies are over-engineering it. You don't need to turn your company into Google 2.0 in order to retain Millennials. Sometimes, all we need is the go-ahead to invest some time and energy in a goal or project we care about."

7

Millennial Women—Empowered on the Outside, Left Wanting on the Inside

R ight out of college, Rachel* won a dream job at a global investment bank in New York. She joined the bank's rotational program, serving six months in each of four business functions: collateral management, product development, market sales and trading, and global compliance. Eager to prove herself, Rachel put in fourteen-hour days and eighty-hour weeks, forsaking a life outside of work. Having taught herself how to code at an early age, she developed systems from the ground up for front-, mid-, and back-office processes. In her final rotation, she managed a billing project that demanded massive technical fixes. "People told me I should focus on making vice president, when I hadn't even made associate yet," she recalls, "because I'd been given huge responsibility and delivered on it."

When the rotational program ended, Rachel was promoted from analyst to associate. She felt valued and recognized; the sacrifices she'd made felt amply justified. She believed that as long as she continued to add value, within two years she'd make vice president.

But since her promotion, the path forward—along with the prospect of a leadership role—has grown murkier. Her female colleagues, who are mostly in their early- to mid-thirties, have tagged her as The Millennial: someone whose expectations are outsized relative to her actual abilities and experience. "I started to hear from older people that I was getting ahead of myself," Rachel explains. "The head of global compliance—the same woman who told me I should focus on making VP—accused me of wanting to run before I could walk. And she wasn't the only one."

In response, Rachel has adopted a more self-effacing demeanor. "I've learned to keep my head down a bit," she says. "I said to the business head, 'I'm doing the same job as an executive director and I'm not being compensated like one,' but I said it once, not continually. I don't need credit. I assume it will come to me when it's due. I love working here. But I do find it weird that, for someone who's working eighty-hour weeks, I can't afford dry-cleaning."

Like many Millennial women we interviewed, Rachel, a women's college graduate, has fully internalized Sheryl Sandberg's message. She is leaning in; she is driving pedal-to-the-metal, intent on making a difference in a way that can be seen, felt, and acknowledged. She loves her work. She loves being part of a best-in-class team. She has no desire to work for a smaller company or go out on her own.

But some of the wind propelling her has gone out of her sails. She doesn't mention her management aspirations to her superiors; she's no longer sure that leadership is where she belongs. "I am not trying to take anything from others," she says. "I'm not trying to be a leader. I just want to be part of the team."

EXPECTANT, BUT NOT EMPOWERED

Millennial women enter the workforce fully expecting to fulfill their ambitions, whether that means becoming experts in their fields or attaining positions in senior management. More than Gen X and Boomer women, the Millennial women we interviewed entered the workforce with career aspirations on par with those of their male peers. As CTI's 2009 report *Bookend Generations* revealed, 96 percent of Millennial women crave an intellectually challenging workplace (compared to 98 percent of Millennial men) and 89 percent value a steady rate of advancement and promotion (compared to 94 percent of Millennial men).[56]

Millennial women have good reasons for their great expectations. A steady barrage of empowerment messages—from girl-power ads on TV (e.g., Pantene, Verizon, and Goldieblox), to celebrity-backed campaigns on social media (#BanBossy being but one example), to prime-time shows on major networks (CBS's *Madam Secretary* and *The Good Wife*)—assures them that they are not only empowered but also entitled to power. Millennial women have made Lean In circles a viral phenomenon and can be counted on to flock to gatherings of like-minded careerists. In 2014, Bizzabo, the event management site, listed "13 Empowering Conferences No Woman Should Miss"; in 2015, the list had grown to eighteen, featuring events with global pull like TED-Women, S.H.E. Summit, and WEN (Women's Empowerment Network) Women's Conference.[57] At every turn, from every source, Millennial women have been exhorted to dream big, reach high, and take no prisoners.

Once hired into the corporate lattice, however, disillusionment sets in. We find among Millennials without financial privilege in our sample that women ages thirty and over are *three times as likely* as those under thirty to believe they could never, no matter how high-performing or qualified, achieve positions of power at their companies. And these women ages thirty and over are *six times as likely* to feel that way as the same age group of Millennial white men without financial privilege.

That women come into a firm stoked with ambition and lose steam over time is not a new story. Indeed, in *Women Want Five Things,* we found that women between the ages of thirty-five and fifty are considerably less interested in a top job than women between the ages of twenty-one and thirty-four.[58] But what's dramatically different among Millennial women in the thirty-and-over cohort is how little interest, relative to thirty-and-over Millennial men, they express in a top job: 5 percent vs. 20 percent say they aspire to a powerful position with a prestigious title. Nor do they aspire, relative to men (13 percent vs. 33 percent) to make significant contributions to their fields or professions.

It's a conundrum that has talent specialists scratching their heads. Given the confidence building that Millennials have been subjected to their entire lives, it's mystifying why women like Rachel walk in the door ready to charge to the top only to succumb to a shortfall of confidence barely two steps off the starting block. "With some Millennial women I've mentored over the years, I've noticed a lack of confidence that's surprising to me," remarks Rosemarie Lanard, chief diversity officer at S&P Global. "This generation is a highly valuable pool of talent, and they represent a group of women who, through greater confidence, can help make gender equity in the workplace a tangible reality."

Lisa Westlake of Moody's has observed that some Millennial women in particular would benefit from better knowledge of how to ask for what they want— an important skill to avoid lagging behind their male counterparts. Educating Millennial women on how (and how not) to ask for what they want, prep for important meetings with senior leaders, and build the relationship capital needed for advancement are priorities for Westlake's team. "We should leverage Millennial women's innate self-assurance and ambition while teaching them how best to take action," she says. "Knowing how to go about getting what you want in itself breeds the self-confidence that you can achieve it."

Westlake's point cuts to the heart of the issue. Employers see Millennial women as the key to closing the gender gap, capitalizing on the struggles of first- and second-wave feminists to at last take the helm. But they also see that these women often lack the confidence and know-how required to push through to the top.

External research affirms their observations. In *The Confidence Code: The Science and Art of Self-Assurance—What Women Should Know*, Katty Kay and Claire Shipman explain that women—particularly young women—are highly susceptible to a "confidence gap," which they define as the rift between our ambitious career goals and confidence in our abilities to achieve them. "The confidence gap is an additional lens through which to consider why it is women don't lean in," they write. "Even when we are prepared to tolerate the personal disruption that comes with aiming high, even when we have plenty of ambition, we fundamentally doubt ourselves."[59]

A DEARTH OF ALLIES AND ROLE MODELS

Our research suggests that seeds of self-doubt take root early in Millennial women's careers for a very simple reason: senior women and men do not provide the support, guidance, and inspiration these women need to navigate the corporate labyrinth.

From our interviews with Millennial women, it's apparent that, upon entering the workforce, they're stunned to learn that the path upward is riddled with pitfalls and tripwires they associate with their mothers' or grandmothers' employment experiences. The meritocracy that propelled them to the tops of their classes in college, and which earned them choice internships, rotations, and recruiters' attention, turns out to be as irrelevant to their advancement as their SAT scores. Exuding ambition does not earn them ongoing professional development, nor the attention of executives, nor opportunities that translate into promotion. And instead of extending a helping hand, their presumed allies—senior women—expect them to pay their dues.

"The message is, 'I had it tough so you should too,'" Rachel explains, recalling the reaction among her female superiors to her early career progress. While the senior women in her department initially cheered her on, they changed their tune when they perceived her moving up the ranks more quickly and easily than they had. Rachel was naïve, her female colleagues said, for believing the fast promotions would continue, and they took it upon themselves to curb her expectations. "I get that some of it is about adapting to the corporate environment, where it's not necessarily a meritocracy and things *won't* get handed to you on a silver platter just because you work hard," Rachel says. "But if you want more women leaders, why slow down a woman who's getting ahead? The messaging has gotten kind of mixed." Indeed, instead of helping her prepare for the slings and arrows of corporate leadership, her colleagues' attitudes have caused her to withdraw.

Millennial women grasp the importance to their career progression of proving their mettle and building relationships with powerful leaders—but many, like Rachel, still seek environments in which merit is prized over powerful networks. They work hard to deliver on their job responsibilities, avoiding the office politics that they see as defining many high-level roles. "I look up and see that the people in high-level roles got there because they pulled the right strings," explains Rachel. "It's discouraging."

If Millennial women acquire a dim view of powerful positions, it may well be because the few women they see in those positions model a set of choices they want no part of.

Millennial women we interviewed describe the horror of going to women's events at their firms and hearing senior women asked to describe how they negotiate the demands of work and home. "It can be tough to make time for family," one panelist will confess. "I usually go home at six to get my kids ready for bed, then I head back to the office to keep working so I can keep up with my male colleagues." The next panelist will explain that she gets into work at four a.m. in order to leave early—at eight p.m. Another might explain that, as a single mother, she has to employ two full-time nannies to get the coverage she needs at work. Invariably, one will share that she's elected not to have children because her job is so demanding. "I have so little free time as it is—I'd rather use it to blow off steam at the gym or get some rest when I can!"

Millennial women come away questioning, as anyone hearing these war stories might, whether a top job can possibly be worth it. Hannah,* a twenty-nine-year-old project manager at a tech firm, attended a panel for women leaders in Science, Engineering, and Technology (SET) thinking precisely that. "I was listening to these really successful, really high-ranking women talk about how awful their lives were—how they had to work three times as hard as the men to be recognized and compensated fairly, how they didn't have time to have families, how they barely had time to take care of their own health," she says. "During the Q&A, I got up and asked really bluntly, 'If things are so bad, why should any of us aim to be an executive? What exactly has feminism changed for the better?'" Hannah remembers that the room went completely silent at her question. "They were shocked. No one knew what to say."

Millennial women like Hannah, raised under the banner of '90s Girl Power, falter in their ambition because the senior women ahead of them appear obliged to conform to pale-male norms of executive presence. They're weighed down by unreasonable demands on their time, oppressed by the inability to balance work and family, and not particularly joyous about the power they wield. To Millennial women looking up the corporate chain, achieving a top leadership position looks more like a prison to be avoided than liberation to celebrate. As exemplified by Anne-Marie Slaughter in her viral 2012 *Atlantic* article, senior leaders are sending the message that women simply can't "have it all"—and Millennial women are listening.[60]

Of course, senior women alone are not to blame. The "all pain no gain" messaging comes from top male leaders just as much as—if not more than—their female counterparts. A leader in pharmaceutical sales shared her struggle to promote women in her sales force up to the regional director level, a job held overwhelmingly by men. After commissioning a study to better understand what was holding back high-potential women, she learned that the men in director roles would brag of their sixteen-hour days and weekends spent on the road away from their families—despite the fact that their jobs didn't actually require a 24/7 commitment nor constant overnight travel. "But clearly they enjoyed talking about the heroic measures they took," she told us. "Their talk of sacrifice and hardship was all part of maintaining a macho culture they'd established among themselves—guys one-up each other with this kind of 'endurance contest' conversation. Whereas their female direct reports were listening to this in all seriousness, saying, 'No way is that job for me.'"

Uncertain in their desire to aim for a top job, and finding little support in getting there, many Millennial women like Joy and Hannah find their ambition and opportunities for advancement drying up as they reach a critical point in their careers: they're not looking to exit, but they're not looking to get ahead either—leaving many directionless and disengaged. As Rachel describes her current career aspirations: "I'm an empty vessel."

8

Older Millennials—The Lost Generation

By the time Serge Agroskin joined Moody's Analytics, he was already well established in his career. He had started at his first company, a travel technology firm similar to Expedia, as a software developer, but within the first year was supervising a team of engineers in developing the firm's proprietary hotel and vacation products, updating its payment system, and piloting a web service. Overall, he handled a portfolio of products worth more than $60 million in annual revenue. Agroskin left the travel firm to team up with a spinal surgeon; together they started a healthcare technology venture specializing in online orthopedic education. "There was nothing like it on the market yet," Agroskin recalls. "The entire platform had to be built from the ground up." The startup was a success: through word-of-mouth, their user base swelled to over seventy thousand registered surgeons with millions of monthly page views, making their website a leading online destination in orthopedic education—and a hot target for acquisition. When his partner backed away from a lucrative offer, Agroskin considered the opportunity that Moody's offered him: to be the lead developer on a product line in the analytics division that they wanted to build from scratch in two years' time. Excited by the challenge, Agroskin signed on. Before the two years were up, the product line that he and his team developed had increased sales in analytics by several million dollars.

Now working in Moody's San Francisco office, Agroskin is a director of software architecture, managing fifteen engineers in the firm's platform-engineering group, and charged with overseeing the construction of a platform for over thirty products.

He is thirty-one years old.

THE INVISIBLE LEADERS IN YOUR MIDST

Today's managers—and tomorrow's corporate leaders—aren't kids. But they *are* Millennials: 62 percent of the Ninety-One Percent between the ages of thirty and thirty-four are, like Agroskin, in management. These older Millennial managers are well on their way to executive leadership; some 8 percent are already there.

Among senior leaders and HR professionals, the Millennial moniker is so reflexively associated with the twenty-something crowd that the very idea of a thirty-something Millennial doesn't register. "To be honest, I don't hear much conversation around the different age segments within Millennials," admits Rosemarie Lanard, chief diversity officer at S&P Global. "Millennials are usually referenced as a group, so the upper and lower ends of the generation get combined." And, she agrees, the lumping skews impressions towards the younger end of the spectrum. "A lot of what available, broad-based research has shown—that they don't marry, buy houses, or have children—leads to a perception that they're not interested in the major life events that have traditionally defined other generations. To be fair, we shouldn't equate this in the workplace with lack of interest in advancing," she says.

Millennials are indeed holding off on marriage, children, and homeownership (or forgoing them entirely) more so than previous generations.[61] This does not mean, however, that all Millennials are unencumbered by familial commitments. In fact, we find that a significant number of Millennials without financial privilege *do* have partners and children—and this is particularly true of Millennials at the upper age range of this cohort. Three-quarters (75 percent) of Millennials ages thirty and over are married or living with partners (compared to 55 percent of Millennials under thirty), and 51 percent have children (compared to 26 percent of Millennials under thirty).

A majority of older Millennials without financial privilege, that is, have significant responsibilities at home, as well as on the job. Yet, it's a mistake to assume that even those Millennials without partners or children are stuck in perpetual adolescence—or should be viewed through the same lens as is applied to their

younger peers, dismissed as "kids" when they are anything but—and it's a perception they understandably
resent. Those we interviewed sought to distance themselves from the under-thirty representatives of their
generation.

"I don't relate to my younger Millennial colleagues,"
asserts a thirty-two-year-old manager working in the
healthcare industry. "There's a lack of maturity in the
way they behave in the office that I don't identify with."
A thirty-four-year-old expresses frustration that her
manager continually compares her to his twenty-three-
year-old daughter. "True, I'm not married and I don't
have kids—my lifestyle is the same in that regard,"
this Millennial points out. "But I grew up with card
catalogues and cassette tapes; I still keep a hardcopy
planner. Frankly, I have more in common with most
Gen Xers and Boomers than I do with Millennials right
out of college." She wishes that management could
focus on her track record instead of the choices she's
made in her personal life. "Isn't who I am on the job,"
she challenges, "more important than who I am in my
off-time?"

Older Millennials yearn for their leadership potential to be evaluated on the basis of their professionalism,
commitment, and achievements in the workplace—not
on the basis of their generational demographic or the
lifestyles they've chosen. As Agroskin puts it, "For me,
showing maturity as a manager and a leader is about

building the best possible product with my team. I want to be judged on the quality of my work. That's it."

But our data reveals that employers persist in seeing these accomplished managers as though they were twenty-four. In our non-financially privileged cohort, just 21 percent of these older Millennials say they have both rewarding relationships and intellectual growth and challenge in their careers—an even lower percentage than Millennials under thirty, 26 percent of whom have both rewarding relationships and intellectual growth and challenge in their careers. While 64 percent of older Millennials value support from colleagues in getting their work done, just 28 percent say they have this aspect of rewarding relationships on the job (compared to 42 percent of Millennials under thirty). Two out of three (66 percent) older Millennials yearn to achieve skill mastery/subject matter expertise, yet fewer than one out of three (31 percent) feel they have achieved it. This lack of depth in skill building, compounded by a dearth of supportive workplace relationships, would appear to be a recipe for career stagnation, as our interviewees tell it.

Laurie,* a thirty-four-year-old manager with a large insurance firm, is a case in point. When she was hired out of college in 2005, she qualified for the firm's financial rotation program; after finishing the rotation, she received excellent training from the audit department. But by the time she had worked her way up to a team lead position in the firm's corporate business development unit, investment in her intellectual growth and leadership potential had dwindled and become far less relevant to her current career aspirations. The networking events and learning programs on offer seem tailored to professionals at the very starts of their careers, not for those nearly ten years in. Worse yet, training in leadership and personnel management is nonexistent. With four direct reports and numerous projects going simultaneously, Laurie is scrambling to acquire the managerial skills her current role requires.

"My role changed significantly when I took on the team lead position," says Laurie, acutely aware of her skills deficit. "It's my first role with direct reports, two of whom were *very* hard to work with in the beginning. I didn't have any direction, so I floundered a lot at first."

In addition to deepening her managerial skills, she realizes she needs to broaden her functional skill set. "My function is narrow, and I'm at a point where I can't go much further without crossing over into a different unit," she explains. "I know I need to network more at the senior level and expand my skill set in order to move forward, but when I bring this up with my manager, he says I'm too young to worry about getting pigeonholed."

Nor is it just her manager who sees her this way. Despite all the client relationships she's handled, Laurie finds herself grouped with the interns whenever leaders organize networking events or workshops. That leaders do not see her as an emerging leader raises questions for her about how much more she should invest in her career at the firm. "How old do I have to be," she muses, "for people to see me not as a *future* leader, but as one *right now*?"

It's a question that resonates with virtually all of the older Millennials we interviewed, including thirty-year-old Karen,* who recently left the pharmaceutical industry to work for a medical technology startup. While Karen's first manager took her under his wing, providing her with the high-profile projects and exposure she needed to move up the ranks, that level of support dwindled as she progressed into the murkier realms of middle management. "I was super ambitious and gung-ho to network with senior people," she recalls of those years in pharmaceuticals, "but I couldn't get traction."

Indeed, while the majority (54 percent) of older Millennials recognize that it's important to have relationships with colleagues who can help them advance in their careers, just 21 percent have this critical aspect of rewarding relationships on the job. That is a startlingly low percentage, but especially in comparison with Millennials under thirty, 37 percent of whom say they have colleagues helping advance them in their careers.

Since, as we've seen, senior-level support and sponsorship are crucial to career advancement, this number should send shivers down the spines of corporate succession planners. Older Millennials are the talent pool from which companies will select replacements for exiting Boomers, as Gen X candidates are in short supply. Yet our data shows that ambitious and accomplished older Millennials like Laurie and Karen are flying under the radar of talent management, desperate to find the stretch assignments, leadership development, and sponsors they know they need to succeed at the roles they will inherit.

As Karen concludes, "There's no question that we are the new leaders. But are we being set up for success? That's what keeps me up at night."

PART THREE: THE ASIA-PACIFIC IMPERATIVE

O ctober 7, 2014 was a fateful day in history: the *Financial Times* broke the news that China had overtaken the US as the world's largest economy.[62] But for those keeping close watch over the shifting tides of global commerce, the news came as no surprise.[63] Companies have been expanding their footprints—and talent pools—in the Asia-Pacific region since the early 1980s. By 1990, Asia accounted for 23 percent of world gross domestic product (GDP); by 2014, that number had risen to nearly 40 percent, accounting for more of the world's productivity than either the United States or the European Union.[64] And while, initially, low-skilled factory work described much of the region's economic activity, by 2013, over 40 percent of complex electronics manufacturing came from AsiaPac countries.[65] Mergers and acquisitions by companies in these emerging markets rose by more than 60 percent in 2013 to $37 billion; by 2015, Asian companies accounted for 190 of the global Fortune 500.[66]

AsiaPac is a region of particular importance to companies whose futures depend on penetrating lucrative markets well beyond their own. As a result, multinational corporations (MNCs) are investing significantly in growing their Asian workforces. According to a 2012 *Wall Street Journal* analysis, three-quarters of new jobs at MNCs had come from abroad.[67] Southeast Asia in particular is seeing a boom in recruitment, as companies relocate back-office operations.[68] MNCs have good reason to focus AsiaPac recruitment on Millennials: by 2020, more than 60 percent of all men and women born after 1980 will reside in the AsiaPac region.[69] "Asia and Latin America are where we see the highest concentration of Millennials in our workforce," reveals Nancy Testa, chief diversity officer at American Express. "In these two regions, they represent well above fifty percent of our workforce." And these young men and women will soon be among the most educated in the world: those in China and India alone will account for 40 percent of all tertiary degrees granted to Millennials by the year 2020.[70]

As with recruitment in the US, however, companies rushing to win AsiaPac Millennials just aren't spending on training, developing, and growing this talent into future leaders: AsiaPac accounts for just 20 percent of the global training market.[71] And, it turns out, employers view these Millennial hires through the same clouded lens they apply to new hires in the US.

Global data that we've harvested through our 2016 multimarket survey of 11,936 college-educated men and women working full time in eleven critical markets, including China, Hong Kong, India, the Philippines, and Singapore, reveals that most of the stereotypes heaped upon Millennials in the US simply do not apply to Millennials in AsiaPac countries. We do find that, as with the majority of US Millennials, AsiaPac Millennials want career stability: just 13 percent of them plan to leave their current employers within the year. Chinese Millennials appear to be the stickiest, with only 5 percent looking to move on from their current jobs within the year.

In other ways, Millennials from different countries *within* the AsiaPac region resist sweeping generalizations. They define success differently; they encounter different challenges. With an eye to giving talent specialists a better picture of this rising class of leaders, we provide findings from China, Hong Kong, India, the Philippines, and Singapore.

9

China

Chinese Millennials are here to stay: just 5 percent say they plan to leave their current positions in the next year, and nearly two-thirds (61 percent) do not feel stalled in their careers. Yet these encouraging numbers hide a talent crisis coming down the pike: intergenerational conflict is dealing a blow to Millennials' abilities to gain visibility and build the key relationships with senior leaders that will grow their leadership potential.

While 82 percent of Chinese Millennials want recognition on the job, many feel disconnected from those senior colleagues and leaders who are best placed to advocate for their career advancement. Part of this disconnect may stem from simple lack of face time: 21 percent of Chinese Millennials say that having no face-to-face contact with leaders has made it difficult to build connections with these potential senior advocates, and 30 percent point to senior leaders knowing very little about their work accomplishments as a source of the problem. But 22 percent simply do not feel comfortable building relationships with senior leaders at their companies—double the percentage in most other markets we surveyed. Probing the source of this statistic, our interviews reveal that the rift between Chinese Millennials and their older colleagues and managers is far wider and more barbed than we had anticipated.

A GENERATION APART

To those of Boomer-age in China, the *balinghou* or "Post-'80s Generation" (as Millennials are often described), were born into affluence and comfort. Spoiled by cushy schools and over-attentive parents, Millennials' upbringing could not be more alien to a generation raised during the tumultuous period of the Cultural Revolution, who spent their own early twenties laboring on remote farms.[72] "Older people think that young people don't respect them," says one recent college graduate working at a healthcare consulting firm. "They feel that we are selfish, and that we don't take care of our parents or family as we should."

From the Millennial perspective, the debt owed by children to parents and elders—one of the Confucian principles that survived China's cultural upheaval—is constricting. "The tension is between wanting to get ahead and do what's best for *me*, versus doing what my parents want," observes June,* a Millennial consultant specializing in management psychology. The individualism and self-actualization Chinese Millennials like June value in their careers has become a particularly bitter source of generational conflict, as it clashes not only with Confucian views of filial piety but also with the communist ideals drummed into older generations from an early age. She experienced the backlash firsthand when it came time to choose her major at university: June's family was insistent that she pick a "safe" subject, like finance or computer science, but June had her heart set on psychology. They eventually came to a compromise: she would study psychology, but also business management to hedge her bets. "I was lucky because my dad was supportive of me," June reflects. "Otherwise, it would have been very hard to take a less traditional path and do something I love."

The financial burden on Millennials like June has been exacerbated in recent years by demographics: while for previous generations, familial expectations were spread among several siblings, the One Child Policy has made Millennials the sole focus of their parents' attention.[73] "The One Child Policy has created this 'little princeling' phenomenon," explains a Chinese-American Millennial currently working for an international bank in Shanghai. "Parents and grandparents pour all their resources and attention into one kid, and when that kid grows up, they're expected to provide for their elders financially for the rest of their lives."

Of course, these expectations fall upon Millennial men and women differently. "If you're only allowed to have one kid, most Chinese families would prefer that child to be a boy. Boys are seen as more able to support their parents financially and to continue the family line," this Millennial expat points out. "The problem now is that there's an overabundance of men in the Millennial age range, so young men looking to marry and start a family are struggling." The gender imbalance stemming from the One Child Policy may factor into the perception of gender roles in the workplace and at home, as well: 92 percent of Chinese Millennials agree that in their culture, fathers who are breadwinners are perceived to be better fathers. "There's a lot of societal pressure to find a well-paying job, marry, and buy a house once you reach your late twenties," agrees Yu,* a twenty-nine-year-old contractor at a construction firm in Guangzhou. Yu, who is single himself, understands that pressure all too well. "It's not just family. My colleagues and boss also ask why I haven't settled down yet."

With so many Millennials under incredible pressure to secure safe jobs with steady incomes, it comes as little surprise that 66 percent consider high compensation very important in their careers, and that 63 percent have asked for raises. But recent economic turbulence has dealt a blow to Chinese Millennials' confidence in their future economic success—and, perhaps, eroded their confidence in the job market as well.[74] Taking the risk to chase after their dream careers simply may not seem worth it to Chinese Millennials tasked with providing for their parents and families. "Money is an important factor. I want to be able to maintain my lifestyle without worrying my parents," Yu says, admitting that if he could he would prefer to pursue a career in design. For now, however, he's planning to stay where he is. "I don't love my job, but it's safe."

10

Hong Kong

Grace,* a corporate event planner who manages PR for a Hong Kong-based confectionary, used to love her job. But punishing hours and inadequate financial resources have her entertaining notions of leaving. "I work twenty-four-seven and I'm *still* barely able to afford rent and basic living expenses," Grace says. "I can't save. How will I buy a house or start a family?"

Grace is hardly alone in her worries: a full 65 percent of Millennials in Hong Kong feel similarly stuck and stalled in their careers. Unable to see a future at her current job but without the financial means to walk out, Grace voices many of the concerns raised by the Hong Konger Millennials we surveyed—the majority of whom identify quality of life (58 percent) and high compensation (55 percent) as very important to them in their careers. If Grace's experience is any indication, however, these Millennials aren't entertaining notions of living grandly. The cost of living in Hong Kong has skyrocketed in the past thirty years, intensifying the extremes of economic inequality.[75] "In Hong Kong, wealth is really in your face, and sometimes it creates these wild juxtapositions," recalls Ben,* an expat working at the Hong Kong branch of a major US bank. "I'll walk out of the office and see a two-hundred-thousand-dollar Ferrari driving down the street next to an old lady pushing a wooden cart full of seafood."

Despite a booming economy, more than one million Hong Kong residents currently live below the poverty line, while the top 1 percent of the population has a combined net worth that equals nearly 80 percent of the territory's GDP.[76] "There's a simmering anger over the fact that only the super-rich can afford a good lifestyle here, the same anger that fueled the protests of the Umbrella Movement," says Ben, recalling the student-led, peaceful protests for greater civil liberties and social mobility in 2014.[77] "Young people in Hong Kong feel like they're working hard to line other people's pockets," Ben says. "And they're not wrong."

Hong Kong is the third most expensive city in the world for renters, many of whom are Millennial-age; the average monthly rental cost in Hong Kong is US$1,940 (HK$15,074) per month, while in New York, it's about US$2,630 (HK$20,435).[78] But Hong Kong trails New York in terms of average income. The median college-educated Millennial Hong Konger makes just US$16,772 (HK$130,320) per year, compared to the median US Millennial's US$45,478 starting salary out of college.[79] In fact, salaries for recent college graduates in Hong Kong have *decreased* by 17 percent since 1993.[80] Hours of work in Hong Kong simply don't add up to those in New York: an employee in Hong Kong can purchase an iPhone 6 by working fifty-two hours, while New Yorkers need put in only twenty-four hours to afford one.[81]

HARDWORKING, UNDERVALUED

Perhaps as a result of the depressed rate of compensation, Hong Kong is the hardest-working city in the world, with employees putting in over fifty hours per week on average. That number rises even higher for those in white-collar jobs.[82] The Millennials we surveyed are feeling the burn of these long hours: of the 23 percent who plan to leave their current jobs within a year, one in four (25 percent) cite lack of respect for personal time as a reason for their departure.

It bears noting that Millennials anticipate making a trade-off between compensation and quality of life. "I expect higher compensation, because my job is one that requires putting in very long hours at the office," says one native Hong Konger, who clocks over eighty hours a week at the law firm where he works. "My friends working in other industries don't get paid as much, but they have much better work-life balance—not just shorter working hours, but more flexibility and control over their workflows—so they're willing to take lower pay."

Raymond,* who used to work for a multinational publishing company, says that years of spending evenings and weekends camped at his desk certainly factored into his decision to leave his job, but admits that the hours at his current job as an account manager for an advertising agency aren't much better. The difference? "My time matters here," Raymond explains. "I wasn't seeing any evidence of career advancement at my old job. I'd been working in the same role, with the same pay and the same title for more than five years. It didn't seem to matter that I worked overtime and performed well. Now, when I give one-hundred-fifty percent on a project, my manager notices—and my compensation reflects that." In other words, Millennial Hong Kongers like Raymond are looking for a happy medium: long hours might be made tolerable by higher compensation and greater recognition; lower pay, by greater quality of life.

Compounding the long-hours problem is a cultural emphasis on "face time" at the office. Interviewees like Raymond resent having to put in hours merely, as he puts it, "for the optics." There's an unspoken rule in a lot of Hong Kong companies, one young expat explained, that employees don't leave the office before their managers. "Many of my colleagues, particularly those born and raised in Hong Kong, find it hard to leave before the boss. They end up sitting at their desks doing basically nothing while they wait for managers to go home. It's a huge waste of time and resources, both for employees and for the companies."

Another source of generational conflict in the office stems from technology. Companies may think that Millennials are naturals when it comes to tech skills—and thus don't need training or support to jump on the high-tech bandwagon. Our findings reveal this assumption to be wrong: 92 percent of Hong Konger Millennials say they do not consider themselves tech savvy. Perhaps as a result, they're not huge proponents of remote work arrangements: just one in four (25 percent) feels that the benefits of working virtually outweigh the burdens, and a mere 8 percent of those who *do* work virtually feel that it gives them work-life balance.

The mistaken assumption that all Millennials have an intuitive grasp on technology can lead to generational friction. "Some of my older colleagues like to approach me for technical support rather than calling our IT help line," one interviewee explained. "It's pretty clear that it's just because of my age since I have no IT training or special skills," he admits. "Most of the time, I end up having to Google their question, or call up IT myself. It can be irritating, especially when someone interrupts me in the middle of a project."

Generational issues are further exacerbated by cultural differences. "Technology, particularly social media, is a lot less conspicuous in Hong Kong than in some other places I've worked, like the US or the Philippines," remarked an interviewee currently working in the financial industry, explaining that employees at his firm use different social media platforms, such as WeChat (or Weixin in Chinese), a messaging platform that functions like a combination of WhatsApp,

Facebook, and Venmo. In Hong Kong, WeChat's user base far exceeds those of Western applications, such as Facebook Messenger. So, this Millennial reveals, when Western companies attempt to cater to Hong Kong Millennials using Western social media platforms, the effort often falls flat.[83]

Millennial Hong Kongers hasten to clarify that keeping them loyal and engaged on the job will require more than slick tech solutions. "Using social media in the office is nice, but it's not going to keep me at my job," Grace observes. "There has to be a baseline level of respect for me as a human being: I have to be paid a salary I can live on; I have to have enough time outside the office to have a life and a family. Having time and money tells me that I'm valuable to my employer, and ultimately *that* is what will make me stay."

11

India

"It's impossible to keep qualified Indian Millennials for more than a year or two," one HR professional we spoke with complained. "The job market is too hot, they're too sought-after."

It's a familiar refrain: Millennials are opportunists, looking for the best pay, the best title, the most flexible working hours. Yet, while some 18 percent of the Indian Millennials we surveyed *are* planning to leave their current jobs within the year, they aren't necessarily leaving for greener corporate pastures.

Take Arjun,* for example, who grew up in the bustling southern city of Chennai and has always been hungry for the chance to make a difference in the field of human resources. "I saw a lot of corruption growing up—not just in the public sector, but in companies, too," he explains. "I wanted to help change that." But once Arjun entered the corporate world, he quickly became frustrated. "Even when it was clear that the old processes were actually hurting productivity and employee retention, there was this reluctance to try new things. I would go to my superior with an idea about how to make a system more efficient—like a way to speed up layoff processing, so an employee wouldn't have to wait three months to receive his or her severance pay," Arjun recalls. "He would listen; sometimes he even told me my ideas were good. But it was just lip service. After a while, I realized nothing would ever come of our conversations. Why bother saying anything? It was pointless."

Like Arjun, who eventually left the company for a firm where he felt his ideas were valued, some 36 percent of Indian Millennials who plan to leave within a year say they are moving on because their insights are not valued, and 28 percent say they have no voices within their companies. In short, Indian Millennials are not running *towards* better benefits or higher salaries so much as they are running *from* management that refuses to acknowledge what they have to offer.

A TALENTED POOL

India is a youthful nation: some two-thirds of the population is under thirty-five.[84] It's also a major and growing source of white-collar talent: by 2020, India's college graduates will outnumber those in the US.[85] Those who came of age during India's economic boom bring to the workplace unmatched skill in technology.[86] They have the cross-cultural experience as well as the desire to succeed abroad: according to Mohit Saxena, a product manager based at the Baxalta office in Gurgaon, navigating India's domestic market, with its twenty-nine separate states (each with its own distinct culture, policies, languages, and economy), turns out to be excellent training for a stint abroad. Thanks to the success of several major political movements in recent years, including the 2010 anti-corruption movement and the still-thriving LGBT rights movement—both of which attracted widespread support among India's youth—Indian Millennials enter the workforce intent on driving transformation both at home and in the world. "We've had opportunities that our parents' generation didn't: better education, more political freedom, and economic prosperity," observes Saxena. "The stereotype is that this has made us spoiled and demanding. But in reality, it's made us ambitious for our country. Now that we have the reins in our hands, we feel empowered to drive the change we want to see in India, and in our careers."

To harness this ambition, employers would do well to provide what Millennials sense is important to their careers. Some 81 percent of the Millennials we surveyed in India say that recognition is very important in their careers, and the same number say they want intellectual growth and challenge. Forty-two percent of Indian Millennials who work at multinational organizations— over four times as many as their US counterparts— have requested global assignments. Nearly half—48 percent—have requested special projects at work.

Millennials whom we interviewed, however, expressed frustration with managers' reticence to invest in their growth. When Preeti,* for example, spoke to her manager about expanding her role as a market analyst to include a research project on economic policy, she instead found herself stuck with even more menial work. "I was really emotionally involved in my job at first," she says. "But it killed my enthusiasm to hear someone senior telling me that I was getting above my place and that I needed to back off."

Generational conflict, that is, serves to keep Indian Millennials from driving the change they embrace so readily. "Many of my older colleagues waited years to gain new responsibilities in their careers," Preeti explains. "People didn't push for more. So when we ask for opportunities, it sometimes doesn't come across well."

12

The Philippines

The first thing Millennials in the Philippines want employers to know is that Millennial stereotypes imported from the US don't apply. "Most of us grew up when life was not so easy," says a twenty-eight-year-old Filipino financial planner based in Manila. "We learned to work hard for the things we wanted, like better quality of life or interesting jobs. We know that our parents and siblings are depending on us to help support them. I think some companies, particularly foreign companies, don't understand that context."

The Philippine economy, though one of the fastest growing in the world, is still very much an emerging market: over 80 percent of the population lives on 250 pesos (about US$5) per day or less.[87] That fact alone helps explain why 90 percent of Philippine Millennial talent prioritize compensation among the things they value most.

Thinette Quilaneta, a twenty-eight-year-old team leader in financial transcript production at S&P Global in Manila, is one of them. As soon as she graduated from the University of the Philippines Diliman, she took a job in a call center, earning enough to provide for herself, her partner, and her infant son. But the rising cost of living in the Philippines forced her to consider a career change. Prices of foodstuffs are some of the most volatile: while Quilaneta had no trouble feeding her household with a five-hundred-peso weekly food budget less than three years ago, today that amount is barely enough to cover two days. So when a position at S&P Global opened, she grabbed it, not only for the significant bump in salary but also—critically for Quilaneta—for the generous health benefits. "I can add up to four dependents for free," she says and uses her policy to cover her mother and sister as well as her child. "In my previous job, only I could have free health coverage. I would have had to pay extra to cover my kid."

Just as vital to Filipino Millennials are opportunities to develop and grow their skills. Nearly all (94 percent) of those we surveyed want their work to provide intellectual growth and challenge, half (50 percent) have requested leadership development opportunities, and of those at multinational organizations, 12 percent have asked for a global assignment, while 8 percent have asked for a rotation at headquarters. "While salary is an important consideration, I ended up choosing the company that I felt would give me the most opportunity to grow as an individual in my career," says a Filipino Millennial employed by a bank that is headquartered in the UK. Although currently working in Manila, he aspires to work abroad in the near future. "I'm working on perfecting my English, because I want to move to HQ," he explains. "I can see that that's the step to take my career to the next level."

Among our interviewees, many articulated a link between growth and international work experience. Several observed that the country's most successful export is its people, a reference to the fact that money sent back home from Filipinos working overseas accounts for as much as 8.5 percent of the country's GDP.[88] Millennials, too, have been shaped by the remittance economy: a recent study found that more than one in five college freshmen have at least one parent working outside the Philippines.[89] "We grew up understanding that money comes from overseas," says a Millennial whose father and sister are both employed in the US. "That's given us a mindset that is more global and more experimental."

Indeed, we find Filipino Millennials are particularly restless: 20 percent plan to stay with their current employers for less than one year. "Working for an international corporation in the Philippines is a proxy for opportunity," one explained to us. "I'm looking for more than an average job working at a call center or fast-food company." Among those we surveyed, 44 percent aren't satisfied with their rates of advancement and almost two-thirds (62 percent) feel stalled in their careers.

LACKING REWARDING RELATIONSHIPS

Twenty-seven-year-old Nimuel* conducts business development for a Filipino conglomerate, a job he perceives will give him career traction in part because of the relationships he's been able to forge with those in charge. "Nothing compares to the training opportunities, mentoring, and promotions that you gain from building those relationships," he says. "Those are core."

In fact, the lack of rapport with senior management at his last job was what prompted Nimuel to leave. His experience is far from unusual: nearly a quarter (23 percent) of Filipino Millennials say they share no social networks with senior leaders at their companies, and nearly one in four (22 percent) say that senior leaders know very little about their work accomplishments. Language barriers can impede building such relationships, as 21 percent concede: across the Philippine archipelago of seven thousand islands, more than seventy-five different languages are spoken. A Millennial born in Cebu, the country's second largest city, might speak Cebuano as her first language, whereas a native of Luzon (the island where Manila is located) might grow up speaking English and Tagalog. "Luzon is very different from the outer islands," observes the Millennial founder and CEO of a social enterprise start-up with operations spread across the Philippines. "It's different culturally and English is widely spoken, which is not as true elsewhere."

Given the geographic, cultural, and language diversity, multinationals' first investment in Filipino Millennials might well be in language training, to create avenues for sponsorship relationships to form. But with Millennials comprising a third of the country's population, investment cannot stop there.[90] "I see a lot of people in my age group making sacrifices for their careers because they want the chance to lead," Nimuel concludes. "We're willing to put in the work, if companies will give us the opportunity."

13

Singapore

As Singapore nears its fiftieth anniversary, the city-state will be hard-pressed to maintain its position as Asia's home for talent. To maintain its GDP growth rate, which has averaged about 7 percent since 1976, the city-state will need to hold onto its Millennials, who make up about 22 percent of the overall population of 5.54 million.[91] But Millennials are impatient with what they see as a repressive management hierarchy. "I've always valued 'working smart,' but when you talk to people of different generations, it's all about 'working hard,'" says Wendy,* an associate at a local advertising agency. This dissonance hit home when she tried to negotiate a raise. "I had been moving up quickly and taking on expanding roles, but my male boss acted like I was asking for things I didn't deserve yet. Then his wife gave me a lecture about how when she was my age, she just took what she could get and said yes to everything. I was shocked that she saw my asking for a raise as tantamount to a 'no.'"

Close to two-thirds (65 percent) of Singaporean Millennials, we find, feel stalled in their careers.

Perhaps as a result, 23 percent are looking to leave their current jobs within the next year. The top three reasons propelling them to jump? Some 28 percent of those who intend to leave within a year say their insights are not valued; 27 percent feel they don't have voices at their companies; and 22 percent feel they're invisible to the power players at their companies.

Feeling alienated and dissatisfied is especially an issue for Singaporean Millennials working at MNCs. In the other markets in our survey, Millennials feel MNCs offer *more* opportunities to grow in their careers. But in Singapore, 67 percent of Millennials at MNCs, as compared to 62 percent at local companies, say they feel stalled in their careers.

BRIDGING HISTORICAL BIASES

One Millennial attributes this sense of sluggish career mobility to the fact that expatriates command disproportionate respect in the Singaporean economy. Although non-ethnic Chinese comprised some 76 percent, Malays about 15 percent, and Indians about 7 percent of the population in 2015, "People look up to white people, especially white expats," this Millennial observes—an enduring bias rooted in Singapore's original identity as a colonial trading post in the British Empire.[92] "It's part of our history that I see playing out in the workplace. Generally, if you're a Western expat, you have instant respect. People listen to you. Otherwise, they ignore you."

Henry,* who works in process improvement at the Singapore office of a UK-based multinational financial services firm, says he's experienced this assumption firsthand. "Whenever I came up with a creative way to fix a problem, I could meet with senior managers in Singapore. They knew me and trusted my advice," he says. But after they approved his suggested solution, it would have to be approved in the UK home office. "Things would get held up. They couldn't find the right people, then they couldn't understand why we needed the change or how to implement the change. Then they had to approve the money for it." He goes on, "Because the UK leaders didn't have a relationship with me, they didn't trust me to know what's best. They always wanted to hire external consultants to verify my work. They made a mountain out of nothing!" Henry is convinced that his employer's lack of communication and transparency hampered his ability to build skills and held back his career advancement.

Salary differences between expats and native Singaporeans are another source of simmering resentment among Millennials. In a city ranked as one of the world's most expensive, compensation is no minor issue; and while the Singaporean government has been tightening restrictions on the employment of overseas nationals in an attempt to push banks to hire more local candidates, tensions around higher expat salaries remain high.[93] Although companies often justify expat compensation based on the lack of social services available to non-citizens in Singapore—expatriates typically don't have access to government-subsidized housing, for example—many Millennials agree that the salary differential has its roots in old biases. "It's based on this colonial mentality," notes one expat Millennial. She continues, "I understand why Singaporeans are bitter."

Despite mounting dissatisfaction, local Singaporean Millennials we interviewed say that working for a multinational company is still seen as a mark of success—particularly by parents. For Millennials, filial respect continues to be a factor in their career trajectories, as Ahmad,* a Singaporean native who currently works for a major multinational bank, explains. "In Singapore, parents play a big role in their children's major life decisions," he says. "It's a follow-your-parents culture, rather than an individualistic culture."

Still, parental influence is waning, eroded by the irresistible power of technology. As the first generation to have grown up in a digital world, Millennials everywhere are comfortable forming connections through social media. Singaporean Millennials, too, are reaching out online and forging career contacts on their own. "You don't need to go through the parental network," comments another Millennial, who is employed at a tech startup. "People question their parents more because they have more access to information through the web. Millennials are more confident that they—not their parents—know what's best for themselves."

Driven by a new generation, change is coming to staid and stable Singapore—and multinational companies looking to attract and retain Millennial talent will need to adjust in order to succeed in a new world. As Henry puts it, "We have our eyes open. We see how things could be better, for our careers and for our companies, so we aren't satisfied with the status quo."

PART FOUR: SOLUTIONS

ACCENTURE—DEVELOPMENT PARTNERSHIPS

"There's a change in the zeitgeist," said Gib Bulloch of the influx of civic-minded Millennials into the corporate workforce. Bulloch, who until recently headed Accenture Development Partnerships (ADP), a nonprofit wing of the global consultancy, doesn't think this shift is a bad thing: as he revealed in a recent interview with the *Financial Times*, the key to unlocking Millennials' passions and innovations in the workplace is to engage with—rather than shrink from—their desire for meaning and purpose. [94]

It was with this insight in mind that Bulloch and his team developed the ADP program, a unique corporate initiative that allows top-performing employees to work in developing countries on consulting projects that help charities in the development sector increase their efficiency and productivity. Accenture supports these executives during their time overseas, covering their placement costs and pay throughout the program (a voluntary 50 percent reduction in salary), while partnering charities pay only a minimal fee to participate. [95]

So far, ADP program participants have completed more than 640 projects around the globe in more than seventy developing countries, contributing over 1.5 million hours of direct work in the field and in excess of $28 million through salary reductions. In recognition of this outstanding work, the program has accrued twenty international awards, accreditations, and nominations.[96]

Yet, while the stated goal of the program is to make Accenture services accessible to development sector organizations at substantially lower market rates than in the private sector, the ADP program has also had a tremendous impact on participating employees as well: a stunning 90 percent of participants believe their experience has helped them develop commercially-relevant skills and accelerated learning. "The opportunity to help Oxfam develop a clear and logical program that will help thousands of people in two different countries is something I will never forget," said Ezra Murad, a senior resources manager, of his experience volunteering through ADP with Oxfam in Sri Lanka and Nigeria.[97]

According to Bulloch, the popularity and impact of the program just goes to show that meaning and purpose is something all employees, from Millennials to Boomers, need at work. "It's about balancing profit with purpose," he observed.[98] Bulloch is not alone in believing the desire for a sense of purpose motivates both younger and more senior employees. "They get challenging work in an exciting environment," agreed Sander van 't Noordende, group chief executive of Accenture Management Consulting. Regardless of what stage an employee is in his or her career, "it is a tremendous leadership development opportunity." [99]

BAXALTA—WORKPLACE OF THE FUTURE: MILLENNIALS' CHOICE

Baxalta may only be a year old—the company spun off from Baxter International in July 2015—but its senior leadership is already planning ahead. "We saw the demographic shift towards a Millennial-dominant workforce just around the corner," says Linda Hartman-Reehl, senior director of diversity and inclusion. "So we decided to design for that future by asking Millennials what changes they would like to see at the new company."

Following the advice of their Millennial talent, Baxalta implemented several daring changes to its structure and workplace culture. First, Baxalta has relocated its hematology division, from its headquarters in Bannockburn, Illinois to downtown Chicago. The space does more than dramatically improve the commute for many of the division's employees—it also provides "hoteling" desk and office space for people in other divisions who live downtown, allowing them to work flexibly instead of traveling to headquarters every day. Along these same lines, Baxalta also created a commuter reimbursement program that will pay up to $130 every month toward commuting expenses for employees who take the train, subway, bus, or ferry; those who incur parking expenses can also cover them by having up to $250 taken out of their paychecks pre-tax. Given that Millennials' pockets tend to be hardest hit by commuting costs, Baxalta's commuter program puts it head-and-shoulders above its competitors in the greater Chicago area.

Further improving the office experience for Millennials, Baxalta has implemented a "Dress for your Day" policy, which allows employees to dress as appropriate for the day's activities—whether that means wearing a suit to meet with a business partner or more casual wear for a day spent at the desk—rather than adhere to a strict corporate dress code. "We trust our employees to make these decisions and not need to have their wardrobes dictated for them," Hartman-Reehl says. "We find they appreciate the autonomy."

In fact, Hartman-Reehl explains, all three of these structural changes are part of the same solution: namely, offering Millennials the opportunity to craft their ideal working environment and maximize their productivity. "We find that giving people the freedom to choose enables performance by creating an environment where all our employees—Millennials, Gen Xers, *and* Boomers—have the comfort level to be themselves."

It is still early to measure the impact of these changes, as they took effect in January of 2016; but anecdotal feedback from Millennial employees has been encouraging. "I've heard two kinds of responses, and both are positive," reveals Hartman-Reehl. "One is that they appreciate being tapped to provide input and shape our future; the other is that they are excited to see that what they've suggested has actually been implemented—it's not just talk." Long run success will be measured by an engagement survey and metrics around retention and ability to attract new Millennial talent. Looking to the future, Hartman-Reehl concludes, "We plan to keep fine-tuning. Rather than just seek out best practices, we're really trying to design the 'next practice' by listening to what Millennials want."

EY—FLEXIBILITY FOR ALL

Ever since the late 1990s, EY has been committed to ensuring all employees have the flexibility they need to succeed, and flexibility continues to be an important part of EY's culture. Yet, with the ballooning number of Millennial managers, integrating workplace flexibility has taken on a new urgency. "It is imperative that we continue to evolve to provide a workplace that shifting generational workforces expect," explains EY's Flexibility Leader Maryella Gockel. In fact, the results of EY's 2015 *Global Generations* study found that 78 percent of Millennials are in dual-career families—versus 47 percent of Boomers—and that 75 percent of Millennials want the ability to work flexibly and still be on track for promotion.

Flexibility at EY comes in two forms: a culture of day-to-day flexibility, also known as "flex for all," and a formal system of flexible work arrangements. The former has chiefly been accomplished, according to Gockel, through the tone from the top: EY is full of visible senior role models who work flexibly. "If everyone is honest about their obligations external to work, especially those in senior positions, you start to get rid of the stigma around not being in the office," explains Gockel. Employees are also encouraged to combine their personal and EY calendars and to be transparent about their needs. Additionally, teams share a calendar and are expected to foster the most flexible work possible for each other while considering client and in-person demands.

This culture of flexibility lays the foundation for successful flexible work arrangements, or FWAs. FWAs are agreements for employees with a regular need for flexibility wherein the employee proposes a business case for a reduced or seasonal schedule, change in hours, compressed workweek, or the ability to telecommute one or more days per week. Once approved, these employees are still on track for promotion and other opportunities. For instance, one employee, who originally intended to leave the firm to study art, was encouraged to instead pursue an FWA. For several years, she worked at a reduced schedule and still progressed from senior manager to partner.

Organization-wide surveys shed light on the value of flex time to EY's workforce: within the top-performing 25 percent of teams, those who say they have the flexibility they need are retained at a rate 6.1 percentage points higher than those who do not. "We're still working to make sure all our people understand that if they're transparent about what they need and specific about how they will achieve it, while still being a high-performing team member and serving our clients, working flexibly will not be a detriment to their career progression," explains Gockel. "As long as the work gets done, it doesn't matter where it gets done or what time of day it's getting done. It's the quality that matters."

GE – PD@GE

General Electric was once famous for its strict employee ranking system, known as "the vitality curve," which graded its employees and fired the bottom 10 percent every year. But while this system enjoyed a vogue in the 1990s under the leadership of then-CEO Jack Welch, views have since changed. "The world isn't really on an annual cycle anymore for anything," explained GE's head of human resources Susan Peters in an interview with *Quartz*. "We think over many years it had become more a ritual than moving the company upwards and forwards." Furthermore, Peters notes, the demographics of GE's workforce have changed drastically, and younger employees take a very different approach to feedback: namely, "more frequent, faster, mobile-enabled."

The new system is forward-thinking on all three fronts. Instead of relying on a single annual performance review, by the end of 2016, GE's three-hundred-thousand-strong workforce will be receiving frequent feedback and occasional rankings via a dedicated mobile application. PD@GE, which stands for Performance Development at GE, will allow managers to delineate near-term goals and priorities on-the-go to keep their direct reports regularly informed on their progress. Employees will also be empowered to give and request feedback to or from anyone in the company—at any time.

Feedback is framed positively: employees and managers are encouraged either to continue doing something, or to consider changing an aspect of their performance—allowing the app to function like a coaching tool. "You know that humans don't really like to give negative feedback, it's just not something that anybody does well," explains Peters. "So if you want the person that's working for you to improve, you have to think about it in true coaching terms."

So far, the app has proven to solve many of the problems it was meant to solve, without disrupting the meritocracy and pay differentiation that GE prides itself on. In fact, Peters anticipates that widespread adoption of PD@GE will actually improve meritocratic career advancement by providing many more metrics of success: while employees will still have annual summary conversations with their managers to reflect on past performance and establish aims for the next year, these performance reviews will be balanced by ongoing evaluation.

The app will also ensure that reviews and feedback flow in both directions, allowing managers to monitor their relationships with direct reports and vice versa. "This allows me to ensure that I'm in a position to change tomorrow," says GE executive Raghu Krishnamoorthy. "But this is just the tool. The most important thing is the conversation. [The app] makes it incumbent on me to be a coach."[100]

MOODY'S—"BRIDGING THE GAP" WORKPLACE MENTORING PROGRAM

Moody's Bridging the Gap Workplace Mentoring Program is the brainchild of Millennial employees involved in Moody's Multicultural Employee Resource Group (ERG). Inspired by President Obama's "My Brother's Keeper" initiative, this Millennial-led taskforce developed the grassroots program in partnership with Big Brothers Big Sisters (BBBS) of NYC to address the achievement gap specific to young black and Hispanic men in the New York area.

"The differentiator is that we're focusing on young men of color, and we're matching them with a diverse group of Millennial mentors—men and women, from all different backgrounds and ethnicities," explains Tiphany Lee-Allen, an assistant vice president at Moody's Investors Service, and a Millennial co-lead of the program. "We wanted to reach this forgotten demographic in a new way." The program was supported by Moody's senior leaders and The Moody's Foundation, as part of their ongoing work to support the needs of the community.

In its inaugural year, Bridging the Gap has connected fifteen male mentees (also known as "Littles") in their sophomore year of high school with Millennial-age mentors at Moody's New York office for biweekly, two-hour sessions. The rigorous vetting process for prospective mentors, which is facilitated by BBBS, includes a background check and interviews followed by a series of training workshops to prepare mentors for various scenarios. Rather than being matched up in pairs (as is typical for mentoring programs), mentors and mentees meet as a group, allowing for connections to grow between all participants rather than just mentors and mentees. "At the start the young men didn't all know each other, so through the program they've made friendships and developed this new support system at school," says analyst Vanessa Youngs, who is herself a mentor and program co-lead. "The same is true on the mentor side."

Sessions focused on a range of topics from effective communication, problem solving, and teamwork, to interview preparation and academic goal setting. In addition, the program brings in Moody's employees to give short thirty-minute presentations on particular topics, such as personal branding, capital market trends, or to describe what it's like to work as an analyst. A dedicated social worker, sourced through BBBS, is on hand at every session should any mentor or mentee need professional support. Moving forward, Bridging the Gap will grow organically by adding new cohorts of mentees yearly. "We'll keep up with the current cohort, and will start with a new cohort of tenth graders each year," Lee-Allen explains. There are also plans in the works to update the curriculum to keep up with the needs of their mentees as they grow through the program, such as providing college-readiness preparation.

While the program will undergo a formal evaluation process once the first cohort of Littles graduates, there are already early indications of success. "Mentees are already asking about our plans for the fall, and we have a waiting list of Moody's volunteers who want to be mentors next year," Youngs reveals. "There's a boost in energy the moment our Littles arrive. That tells me we're doing something right."

NOVO NORDISK—MILLENNIAL ERG

Millennials are a unique and expanding talent pool that Novo Nordisk is interested in better understanding, developing, engaging, and retaining. One way they accomplish this is through the sponsorship of the Millennial Employee Resource Group (ERG).

The grassroots ERG formed less than a year ago and already boasts a membership of nearly five hundred employees. Open to all employees, including older members who are "Millennials at Heart," the ERG is working to bridge Novo Nordisk's diverse, multigenerational workforce to strengthen the company culture, help solve business problems, and benefit patients.

Executive sponsor and CVP of human resources, Jackie Scanlan, explains, "We recognize that our future success hinges on our ability to engage Millennials in a meaningful way that benefits the company and benefits them. Not only are they our future leaders; they also possess valuable perspectives, for instance, in terms of interacting with employees, patients, and our communities in new and interesting ways. We are learning from them every day."

Novo Nordisk Millennials are highly motivated to identify critical business challenges and equally encouraged to jump in to problem solve. "The company clearly supports us and this ERG," says Mike Dill, the ERG's current leader. "So it's particularly exciting to see the contribution we're able to give *back*." With the support of his manager and Novo Nordisk's Diversity and Inclusion Office, Dill has had the opportunity to help shape strategy as well as lead cross-functional and multigenerational teams with the goal of building on the ERG's momentum and leveraging the company's diversity of thought. Dill has recently partnered with the SVP of Sales to participate in discussions across the country around the importance of developing and leveraging talent across generations.

The ERG has already made great strides in bringing both Millennial insights and unique concerns to the forefront of workplace initiatives. In addition to planning networking events, the ERG produces a monthly newsletter featuring Millennials in the workplace and promotes events such as the American Diabetes Association Step Out: Walk to Stop Diabetes®. The group is also working with other Novo Nordisk ERGs to provide their input on the revamp of the company's online mentorship matching portal, which Millennial members agree is vital to the ongoing development of all employees.

"We are deliberately creating an environment where Millennials, and all generations, have the opportunity to work side-by-side with senior executives," shares Scanlan. "Millennials are able to share their ideas and development needs, and our executives are getting a bit of reverse mentoring at the same time. While it's early, we know it is working because leaders are now coming to us and asking how they might engage this ERG in innovation discussions and brainstorming sessions."

PEPSICO — INSIGHTS DATA APP

For years, PepsiCo's Insights team had only one platform for translating consumer data for its marketing and product teams: PowerPoint decks. "It was very transactional," says Stefania Gvillo, VP of consumer strategy and insights at PepsiCo's North American Beverages group, which handles Pepsi, Mountain Dew, Sierra Mist, and numerous other drink brands. The piles of "sixty-page decks, binders, and spreadsheets" were, according to Gvillo, "not very inspiring," not to mention unwieldy and frustrating for marketing and product team leads looking for a specific data point or trend. Adding to the need to change how insights were delivered was an even more pressing issue: Millennials.

"Millennials are here; Gen Z is about to enter the workforce. They communicate and experience content in very different ways," said Gvillo. "They want digestible, quick, and immersive."

So PepsiCo's North American Insights team made a revolutionary decision: to ditch the PowerPoints in favor of the next generation's favorite mode of information delivery—mobile apps. The new app lets Insights teams create and distribute custom-designed content and data to marketing, strategy, and product teams, allowing those teams to quickly locate and download just the content they need. The app hosts eight "publications" that are customized for each consumer brand. Each brand publication is customizable to convey data on the current surveys, reflect consumer attitudes on specific products, and show how brands, products, or ads are performing in different market segments.

The app also incorporates experiential activities and quizzes to make large amounts of data and product information more digestible to employees. Employees aren't penalized if they don't know answers—the function of the testing is to enliven the learning process and keep employees engaged, Gvillo explained. She is also experimenting with data "experiences" and offline events "to engage people, and make [the learning process] fun."

To create the app, PepsiCo worked with StickyDocs, a design agency specializing in innovative data visualization and delivery solutions. "The only way organizations have ever distributed insight is through email and a PowerPoint deck," observed Marcus Jiménez, founder and CEO at StickyDocs. "The practice of data visualization and insights socialization for the workforce is a new concept for many brands." But it's a concept that is vital for corporate leaders to grasp, according to Jiménez, as companies like PepsiCo grow ever more reliant on Millennials (and, soon, Gen-Zers) as both their consumer base and workforce. "It's not just an imperative for brands," he added. "It's inevitable, as workers are demanding it."

Gvillo agreed that the app is an employee-driven innovation, but she also sees the potential for this new, interactive method of sharing Insights team data with the rest of the company to drive significant profit, both through market growth and product development. "We drive decisions that ultimately lead to sustainable growth," she said of her team's impact through the app. "Everything we do impacts the bottom line."[101]

PFIZER—TALENT MARKETPLACE

Hoping to facilitate greater mobility across Pfizer business units and offer unique developmental experiences to colleagues, senior leaders green-lighted the Talent Marketplace initiative in June 2014. Talent Marketplace is a global internal opportunity posting website accessible through the company's intranet that allows any colleague to post or apply for short-term developmental opportunities within Pfizer, ranging from joining a team in a different division for a three-month project to shadowing a senior leader for a day.

"It's inviting and intuitive, and meets a critical need for colleagues and the business," says Senior Director of Performance Excellence Rob Lewis, who oversees the Talent Marketplace interface. Need a project manager? Finding a candidate is as easy as posting the description, location (including "virtual" opportunities), required skills or experience, and duration of the engagement. Depending on the scope of the engagement, colleagues who post opportunities can decide to formally interview candidates or simply connect via email. Colleagues may commit up to 30 percent of their work time to opportunities sourced through Talent Marketplace, approximately 25 percent of which take place entirely virtually for maximum flexibility.

"Developmental opportunities that foster internal mobility are appreciated by employees and lead to greater engagement," explains Lewis. "Talent Marketplace gives Pfizer colleagues a unique opportunity to experience different assignments and different parts of the company."

About half of the Talent Marketplace's four hundred participants seek opportunities within their own business areas, he says, while the other half seek opportunities to explore new skills and areas of business

outside their current responsibilities. Talent Marketplace doesn't just open doors for employees, however;
it also brings project teams and leaders invaluable new
perspectives and problem-solving approaches. "If colleagues are able to develop their skills within their organization or explore roles outside of their teams, the opportunities to create their own change are now at their
fingertips," Lewis notes.

"It's rewarding to know that your employer supports
your development and is open to you trying something
different," comments Tierra Ryan, a participant and
medical writer who spent 15 percent of her time working
with the Global Medical Information team, to which she
hopes to eventually transition. "People evolve, and as
you interact with other divisions, it's natural to develop
an interest in something different," she adds. "Also,
the ability to transition cross-divisionally absolutely
diminishes the likelihood that I'll have to look for a job
outside of Pfizer when I ultimately decide I'm ready for
a new role."

As of July 2015, Pfizer's Talent Marketplace has been
translated into eight languages and incorporates email
alerts, which give participants instant notification when
opportunities that meet their preconfigured criteria
arise. These changes are the direct result of feedback
from a survey built into the site. Lewis anticipates Talent
Marketplace will continue to grow and better serve
those who use it based on continuing feedback. "It's a
truly inclusive development tool," he says. "It doesn't

just target people at a certain level; it gives everyone at Pfizer the opportunity to grow and control their own career trajectory."

ENDNOTES

1. The US Census measures the Millennial generation as those born between 1982 and 2000 ("Millennials Outnumber Baby Boomers and Are Far More Diverse, Census Bureau Reports," United States Census Bureau, June 25, 2015, https://www .census.gov/newsroom/press-releases/2015/cb15-113.html).

2. Sylvia Ann Hewlett and Lauren Leader-Chivée, *The X Factor: Tapping into the Strengths of the 33- to 46-Year Old Generation* (New York: Center for Work-Life Policy, 2011).

3. Richard Fry, "Millennials Surpass Gen Xers as the Largest Generation in US Labor Force," Pew Research Center, May 11, 2015, http://www.pewresearch.org/fact-tank/2015/05/11 /Millennials-surpass-gen-xers-as-the-largest-generation-in-u-s -labor-force/; "Big Demands and High Expectations: The Deloitte Millennial Survey," Deloitte, January 2014, http://www2 .deloitte.com/content/dam/Deloitte/global/Documents/About -Deloitte/gx-dttl-2014-Millennial-survey-report.pdf.

4. "Millennials Outnumber Baby Boomers," Census Bureau (see note 1).

5. The Council of Economic Advisers, "15 Economic Facts about Millennials," Executive Office of the President of the United States, October 2014, https://www.whitehouse.gov/sites /default/files/docs/Millennials_report.pdf.

6. 6.4 percent of Millennials (aged 18-29) vs. 1.9 percent of adults over the age of 65 identify as LGBT (Gary J. Gates and Frank Newport, "Special Report: 3.4% of US Adults Identify as LGBT," Gallup, October 18, 2012, http://www.gallup.com/poll/158066 /special-report-adults-identify-lgbt.aspx).

7. Drew DeSilver, "The Many Ways to Measure Economic Inequality," Pew Research Center, September 22, 2015, http:// www.pewresearch.org/fact-tank/2015/09/22/the-many-ways -to-measure-economic-inequality/.

8. "About," Occupy Wall Street, accessed May 11, 2016, http:// occupywallst.org/about/.

9. Jen Wieczner, "Most Millennials Think They'll Be Worse Off Than Their Parents," *Fortune*, March 1, 2016, http://fortune.com/2016/03/01/Millennials-worse-parents-retirement/.

10. Council of Economic Advisers, "15 Economic Facts" (see note 5).

11. Micah Solomon, "2016 Is the Year of the Millennial Customer: Is Your Customer Experience Ready?" *Forbes*, November 14, 2015, http://www.forbes.com/sites/micahsolomon/2015/11/14/2016-is-the-year-of-the-Millennial-customer-heres-how-to-be-ready/#770a96ee6e72; More so than previous generations, Millennials are highly conscious consumers—in a recent survey, nearly nine out of ten Millennials (89 percent) expressed a preference for products from companies that support their social values (Fred Dews, "11 Facts about the Millennial Generation," Brookings Institution, June 2, 2014, http://www.brookings.edu/blogs/brookings-now/posts/2014/06/11-facts-about-the-Millennial-generation).

12. Doug Harward, "How Big Is the Training Market?" Training Industry, June 6, 2014, https://www.trainingindustry.com/blog/blog-entries/how-big-is-the-training-market.aspx.

13. "Economic Report of the President," The White House, February 2015, https://www.whitehouse.gov/sites/default/files/docs/cea_2015_erp.pdf, 147.

14. The average employee's printing costs their company between $600 and $1,300 per year (*State of the Industry,* Association for Talent Development, 2015, http://www.astd.org/Professional-Resources/State-Of-The-Industry-Report; Caitlin McCool, "How to Reduce Printing Costs by 17%: A Guide to Doing Well and Doing Good by Printing Less," GreenPrint Technologies, September 2008, https://www.printgreener.com/pdfs/GreenPrint%20White%20Paper%20September%202008.pdf).

15. *State of the Industry,* ATD (see note 14).

16. "Investment in Training Remains Strong," PR Web, December 16, 2015, http://www.prweb.com/releases/2015ATDStateoftheIndustry/12/prweb13129145.htm.

17. Joel Stein, "Millennials: The Me Me Me Generation," *Time,* May 20, 2013, http://time.com/247/Millennials-the-me-me-me-generation/.

18. Jean M. Twenge, *Generation Me—Revised and Updated: Why Today's Young Americans Are More Confident, Assertive, Entitled—and More Miserable Than Ever Before* (New York: Simon and Schuster, 2014).

19. Stein, "Me Me Me" (see note 17); Gillian B. White, "Millennials Who Are Thriving Financially Have One Thing in Common," *The Atlantic*, July 15, 2015, http://www.theatlantic.com/business /archive/2015/07/Millennials-with-rich-parents/398501/; Jada A. Graves, "Millennial Workers: Entitled, Needy, Self-Centered?" *US News*, June 27, 2012, http://money.usnews.com/money /careers/articles/2012/06/27/Millennial-workers-entitled -needy-self-centered; Larissa Faw, "How Millennials Are Redefining Their Careers as Hustlers," *Forbes*, July 19, 2012, http://www.forbes.com/sites/larissafaw/2012/07/19/how -Millennials-are-redefining-their-careers-as-hustlers/print/; "Mind the Gaps: The 2015 Deloitte Millennial Survey," Deloitte, 2015, http://www2.deloitte.com/content/dam/Deloitte /global/Documents/About-Deloitte/gx-wef-2015-Millennial -survey-executivesummary.pdf; IBM, *Myths, Exaggerations and Uncomfortable Truths: The Real Story behind Millennials in the Workplace* (Somers, NY: IBM, 2015), http://www-935.ibm.com /services/multimedia/GBE03637USEN.pdf.

20. PwC, *Next Generation Diversity: Developing Tomorrow's Female Leaders* (Dublin: PricewaterhouseCoopers, 2014), https://www .pwc.com/gx/en/women-at-pwc/internationalwomensday /assets/next-generation-diversity-publication.pdf; Lauren Noël and Christie Hunter Arscott, *Millennial Women* (Lexington, MA: ICEDR, 2015), http://www.icedr.org/research/documents/15 _Millennial_women.pdf; Pew Research Center, *On Pay Gap, Millennial Women near Parity – For Now* (Washington: Pew Research Center, 2013), http://www.pewsocialtrends.org /files/2013/12/gender-and-work_final.pdf.

21. Kauffman Foundation, *Young Invincibles Policy Brief* (Kansas City: Kauffman Foundation, 2011), http://www.kauffman.org /~/media/kauffman_org/research%20reports%20and %20covers/2011/11/Millennials_study.pdf; Kauffman Foundation, *Then and Now: America's New Immigrant Entrepreneurs, Part VII* (Kansas City: Kauffman Foundation, 2012), http://www.kauffman.org/~/media/kauffman_org/ research%20reports%20and%20covers/2012/10/then_and _now_americas_new_immigrant_entrepreneurs.pdf; "Landmark Study on Millennials Challenges 'Post-Racial' Myth,"

Race Forward: The Center for Racial Justice Innovation, June 7, 2011, https://www.raceforward.org/press/releases/landmark -study-Millennials-challenges-post-racial-myth.

22. "Beyond.com Survey Uncovers How Veteran HR Professionals Really Feel about Job Seekers from Millennial Generation," Beyond.com, May 28, 2013, http://about.beyond.com/press /releases/Millennials.

23. Jeanne Meister, "Job Hopping Is the 'New Normal' for Millennials: Three Ways to Prevent a Human Resource Nightmare," *Forbes*, August 14, 2012, http://www.forbes.com /sites/jeannemeister/2012/08/14/job-hopping-is-the-new -normal-for-Millennials-three-ways-to-prevent-a-human -resource-nightmare/; Lindsay Gellman, "Millennials: Love Them or Let Them Go," *Wall Street Journal*, May 6, 2015, http:// www.wsj.com/articles/how-employers-wrangle-restless -Millennials-1430818203; Reid Hoffman, "A Solution To Millennials' High Turnover Rate," *Fast Company*, December 1, 2014, http://www.fastcompany.com/3039130/the-case-for -encouraging-short-term-job-commitment.

24. DeSilver, "Economic Inequality" (see note 7).

25. Derek Thompson, "A Giant Statistical Round-Up of the Income Inequality Crisis in 16 Charts," *The Atlantic*, December 12, 2012, http://www.theatlantic.com/business/archive/2012/12/a -giant-statistical-round-up-of-the-income-inequality-crisis-in-16 -charts/266074/.

26. This refers to the market basket of consumer goods and services that the Bureau of Labor Statistics uses to generate the consumer price index (CPI), a measure of the average change over time in the prices paid by urban consumers for said goods and services (Michelle Jamrisko and Ilan Kolet, "College Tuition Costs Soar: Chart of the Day," Bloomberg, August 18, 2014, http://www.bloomberg.com/news/articles/2014-08-18 /college-tuition-costs-soar-chart-of-the-day; "Consumer Price Index Data from 1913 to 2016," CoinNews Media Group LLC, 2016, http://www.usinflationcalculator.com/inflation/consumer -price-index-and-annual-percent-changes-from-1913-to-2008/).

27. Jillian Berman, "America's Growing Student-Loan-Debt Crisis," Market Watch, January 19, 2016, http://www.marketwatch .com/story/americas-growing-student-loan-debt-crisis-2016-01-15.

28. Daniel White, "Millennials Want to See a Trump vs. Sanders Matchup," *Time*, January 11, 2016, http://time.com/4175920 /donald-trump-bernie-sanders-Millennials-poll/.

29. Jamie Dimon and Marlene Seltzer, "Closing the Skills Gap," *Politico*, January 5, 2014, http://www.politico.com/magazine /story/2014/01/closing-the-skills-gap-101478.

30. The expected LPR (labor force participation rate) for workers age 55+ in 2020 is 43 percent, meaning that 57 percent of that population will already be retired from the workforce ("CRR Reports on the Impact of Aging Baby Boomers on Labor Force Participation," Gabriel Roeder Smith & Company, March 11, 2014, http://www.gabrielroeder.com/crr-reports-on-the-impact -of-aging-baby-boomers-on-labor-force-participation/).

31. "Millennials Outnumber Baby Boomers," Census Bureau (see note 1).

32. Sylvia Ann Hewlett, Maggie Jackson, and Ellis Cose, with Courtney Emerson, *Vaulting the Color Bar: How Sponsorship Levers Multicultural Professionals into Leadership* (New York: Center for Talent Innovation, 2012).

33. "Millennials Outnumber Baby Boomers," Census Bureau (see note 1).

34. "Global talent pool" is defined as all graduates of tertiary education (college or university level) in 2012 or the most recent year available, determined by tertiary completion and enrollment levels (reduced by assuming a 33 percent completion rate). "Multicultural" here is understood broadly as graduates outside the US and Western Europe ("Education: Tertiary graduates" and "Education: Tertiary enrollment," UNESCO Institute for Statistics, accessed December 19, 2013, http://data.uis.unesco.org/).

35. Sylvia Ann Hewlett, Melinda Marshall, and Laura Sherbin, with Tara Gonsalves, *Innovation, Diversity, and Market Growth* (New York: Center for Talent Innovation, 2013), 5, 52.

36. Sylvia Ann Hewlett, *Forget a Mentor, Find a Sponsor: The New Way to Fast-Track Your Career* (Brighton, MA: Harvard Business Review Press, 2013), 22-3.

37. Sylvia Ann Hewlett, with Kerrie Peraino, Laura Sherbin, and Karen Sumberg, *The Sponsor Effect: Breaking through the Last*

Glass Ceiling (Boston: Harvard Business Review, 2010); Hewlett et al., *Vaulting the Color Bar* (see note 32).

38. Unpublished data from Hewlett, et al., *Sponsor Effect* (see note 37).

39. Hewlett et al., *Vaulting the Color Bar* (see note 32).

40. Ibid.

41. Derek Thompson and Jordan Weissman, "The Cheapest Generation," *The Atlantic*, September 2012, http://www .theatlantic.com/magazine/archive/2012/09/the-cheapest -generation/309060/; Jacob Davidson, "10 Things Millennials Won't Spend Money On," *TIME*, July 16, 2014, http://time .com/money/2820241/10-things-Millennials-wont-shell-out -for/; Zachary A. Goldfarb, "8 Things Millennials Want—and Don't Want—Show How Different They Are from Their Parents," *Washington Post*, February 28, 2015, https://www.washington post.com/news/wonk/wp/2015/02/28/8-things-Millennials -want-and-dont-want-basically-anything-their-parents-wanted/.

42. Council of Economic Advisers, "15 Economic Facts" (see note 5).

43. Michelle Singletary, "Millennials' Money Misfortune," *Washington Post*, March 15, 2014, https://www.washingtonpost .com/business/Millennials-money-misfortune/2014/03/13 /c6659b1e-aa17-11e3-9e82-8064fcd31b5b_story.html; Jenna Goudreau, "Millennials May Not Be Able to Retire Until Age 73," *Business Insider*, October 23, 2013, http://www.businessinsider .com/Millennials-may-not-be-able-to-retire-until-age-73-2013 -10; Rebecca Rifkin, "Average US Retirement Age Rises to 62," Gallup, April 28, 2014, http://www.gallup.com/poll/168707 /average-retirement-age-rises.aspx?utm_source=retire&utm _medium=search&utm_campaign=tiles; Wieczner, "Most Millennials" (see note 9).

44. Jennifer Wang and Portia Boone, "Millennials and Student Debt," New America, 2014, https://www.newamerica.org /downloads/Millennials_and_Student_Debt.pdf.

45. Jenna Goudreau, "Jobs Outlook 2012: Careers Headed for the Dustbin," *Forbes*, February 7, 2012, http://www.forbes.com /sites/jennagoudreau/2012/02/07/jobs-outlook-disappearing -dying-careers-outsourced-eliminated/2/#608c04482189; "What Are the Strangest New Careers of 2015?" *Parade*, April 8, 2015, http://parade.com/387709/parade/what-are-the

-strangest-new-careers-of-2015/; Jeanne Dininni, "Social Marketing: Career Wave of the Future," Nasdaq GlobeNewswire, September 3, 2013, https://globenewswire.com/news-release/2013/09/03/570883/10046604/en/Social-Marketing-Career-Wave-of-the-Future.html.

46. Barney Ely, "Work That Makes a Difference—Keeping Gen Y Brazil on Board," Hays, November 25, 2014, https://social.hays.com/2014/11/25/work-makes-difference-keeping-gen-y-brazil-board/.

47. "Timeline: Brazil," BBC, August 14, 2012, http://news.bbc.co.uk/2/hi/americas/1231075.stm; Pablo Uchoa, "Remembering Brazil's Decades of Military Repression," BBC, March 31, 2014, http://www.bbc.com/news/world-latin-america-26713772.

48. Benedict Clements, "The Real Plan, Poverty, and Income Distribution in Brazil," Finance and Development, September, 1997, https://www.imf.org/external/pubs/ft/fandd/1997/09/pdf/clements.pdf.

49. Organization for Economic Co-operation and Development, OECD Economic Surveys: Brazil (Paris: OECD Publishing, November 2006), 129, https://books.google.com/books?id=Jb3VAgAAQBAJ&printsec=frontcover&source=gbs_ge_summary_r&cad=0#v=onepage&q&f=false.

50. Kenneth Rapoza, "Brazil's Economy Hasn't Been This Bad Since 1930," Forbes, January 14, 2016, http://www.forbes.com/sites/kenrapoza/2016/01/14/brazils-economy-hasnt-been-this-bad-since-1930/#5b3dd29a7dba; David Biller, "Brazil's Highs and Lows," Bloomberg, May 11, 2016, http://www.bloomberg.com/quicktake/brazils-highs-lows; Corinne Chin and Fabiano Leal, "Why Brazil's Youth Turned against the World Cup," The Week, June 9, 2014, http://theweek.com/articles/446419/why-brazils-youth-turned-against-world-cup.

51. "Young Brazilians Have on Average Profiles on 7 Social Networks, Says Study," globo.com, July 18, 2014, http://g1.globo.com/tecnologia/noticia/2014/07/jovens-brasileiros-tem-em-media-perfis-em-7-redes-sociais-diz-estudo.html.

52. Alex Proud, "Crybaby Millennials Need to Stop Whinging and Work Hard Like the Rest of Us," The Telegraph, December 21, 2015, http://www.telegraph.co.uk/men/thinking-man/crybaby-Millennials-need-to-stop-whinging-and-work-hard-like-the/.

53. At least 60 percent of the population growth in the UK since 2004 has been due to immigration; about 86 percent of immigrants to the UK are foreign-born. ("UK Population Growing Twice as Fast as the Rest of Europe," The Week, June 27, 2014, http://www.theweek.co.uk/uk-news/59178/uk -population-growing-twice-as-fast-as-the-rest-of-europe; "The Latest UK Immigration Figures in 5 Charts," *Financial Times*, February 25, 2016, http://www.ft.com/fastft/2016/02/25/the -latest-uk-immigration-figures-in-5-charts/).

54. This poll, conducted by YouGov in collaboration with the charity Relate, defined youth workers (Millennials) as those between the ages of 25 and 34 (John Bingham, "Lonely Britain: Five Million People Who Have No Real Friends," *The Telegraph*, August 12, 2014, http://www.telegraph.co.uk/news/uknews /11026520/Lonely-Britain-five-million-people-who-have-no -real-friends.html).

55. Aime Williams, "Why Millennials Go on Holiday Instead of Saving for a Pension," *The Financial Times*, February 12, 2016, http://www.ft.com/cms/s/2/94e97eee-ce9a-11e5-831d -09f7778e7377.html #axzz40d50PACh.

56. Sylvia Ann Hewlett, Maggie Jackson, Laura Sherbin, Peggy Shiller, Eytan Sosnovich, and Karen Sumberg, *Bookend Generations: Leveraging Talent and Finding Common Ground* (New York: Center for Work-Life Policy: 2009).

57. Stephanie Brenner, "13 Empowering Conferences No Woman Should Miss," Bizzabo, May 22, 2014, http://blog.bizzabo.com /13-empowering-conferences-no-woman-should-miss; Guy Morag, "15 Empowering Women's Conferences in 2015," Bizzabo, May 26, 2015, http://blog.bizzabo.com/15 -empowering-womens-conferences-in-2015.

58. Sylvia Ann Hewlett and Melinda Marshall, *Women Want Five Things* (New York: Center for Talent Innovation, 2014).

59. Katty Kay and Claire Shipman, *The Confidence Code: The Science and Art of Self-Assurance—What Women Should Know* (New York: HarperCollins, 2014).

60. Anne-Marie Slaughter, "Why Women Still Can't Have It All," *The Atlantic*, July/August 2012, http://www.theatlantic.com /magazine/archive/2012/07/why-women-still-cant-have-it -all/309020/.

61. "Millennials in Adulthood," Pew Research Center, March 7, 2014, http://www.pewsocialtrends.org/2014/03/07/Millennials -in-adulthood/; Alexandra Sifferlin, "Women Keep Having Kids Later and Later," *Time*, May 12, 2014, http://time.com/95315 /women-keep-having-kids-later-and-later/; Chris Matthews, "Young People Can Afford Homes, They Just Don't Want to Be Homeowners," *Fortune*, August 18, 2015, http://fortune.com /2015/08/18/young-people-can-afford-homes-they-just-dont -want-to-be-homeowners/.

62. Chris Giles, "MoneySupply: The New World Economy in Four Charts," FT Alphaville, October 7, 2014, http://ftalphaville .ft.com/2014/10/07/1998332/moneysupply-the-new-world -economy-in-four-charts/.

63. Mike Bird, "China Just Overtook the US as the World's Largest Economy," *Business Insider*, October 8, 2014, http://www .businessinsider.com/china-overtakes-us-as-worlds-largest -economy-2014-10; Chris Giles, "China Poised to Pass US as World's Leading Economic Power This Year," *Financial Times*, April 30, 2014, http://www.ft.com/intl/cms/s/2/d79ffff8-cfb7 -11e3-9b2b-00144feabdc0.html.

64. Akrur Barua, "Packing a Mightier Punch: Asia's Economic Growth among Global Markets Continues," Deloitte University Press, December 18, 2015, http://dupress.com/articles/asia-pacific -economic-outlook-q1-2016-asia-economic-growth-continues/.

65. "Driving Forces behind a Globalized Workforce," SHRM Foundation, 2016, http://futurehrtrends.eiu.com/report-2015 /driving-forces-behind-a-globalized-workforce/.

66. Ibid.; Barua, "Mightier Punch" (see note 66); "Global 500," *Fortune*, accessed May 13, 2016, http://fortune.com/global500/; Claire Groden, "The Fortune Global 500 Welcomes 23 New Members," *Fortune*, July 22, 2015, http://fortune.com/2015/07/22/global -500-newcomers-2/.

67. Scott Thurm, "US Firms Add Jobs, But Mostly Overseas," *Wall Street Journal*, April 27, 2012, http://www.wsj.com/articles /SB10001424052702303990604577367881972648906.

68. "MNCs in Southeast Asia," KPMG, 2015, https://www.kpmg .com/CN/en/IssuesAndInsights/ArticlesPublications/Documents /MNCs-in-Southeast-Asia-The-view-of-multinationals-in -ASEAN-O-201504.pdf.

69. Anastasiia Kolobok, "Millennials: Life-Work Balance of Asian Generation Y," LinkedIn, July 28, 2015, https://www.linkedin .com/pulse/Millennials-life-work-balance-asian-generation-y -anastasiia-kolobok?trk=prof-post&trkSplashRedir =true&forceNoSplash=true.

70. According to the Organization for Economic Cooperation and Development (OECD), if current trends continue, China and India will account for 40 percent of all young people with a tertiary education in G20 and OECD countries by the year 2020, while the United States and European Union countries will account for just over a quarter ("Education Indicators in Focus," Organization for Economic Cooperation and Development, May 2012, http://www.oecd.org/edu/50495363.pdf).

71. Harward, "How Big?" (see note 12).

72. Chinafile, "New School: What's Causing China's Growing Generation Gap?" *The Atlantic*, March 14, 2013, http://www .theatlantic.com/china/archive/2013/03/new-school-whats -causing-chinas-growing-generation-gap/274001/; James Palmer, "The Balinghou," Aeon, March 8, 2013, https://aeon.co /essays /china-s-generation-gap-has-never-yawned-wider.

73. Barbara Demick, "Judging China's One-Child Policy," *The New Yorker*, October 30, 2015, http://www .newyorker.com/news /news-desk/chinas-new-two-child-policy.

74. Katie Allen, "Why is the Global Economy Suffering So Much Turbulence?," *The Observer*, January 23, 2016, http://www .theguardian.com/business/2016/jan/24/why-is-global -economy-suffering-turbulence; "China Fault Lines: Where Economic Turbulence Could Start in 2016," *Bloomberg News*, December 28, 2015, http://www.bloomberg.com/news/articles /2015-12-28/china-fault-lines-where-economic-turbulence -could-start-in-2016; Deloitte, The 2016 Deloitte Millennial Survey, Deloitte Touche Tohmatsu Limited, 2016, http://www2 .deloitte.com/content/dam/Deloitte/global/Documents/About -Deloitte/gx-millenial-survey-2016-exec-summary.pdf.

75. Josh Noble, "Economic Inequality Underpins Hong Kong's Great Political Divide," *Financial Times*, October 21, 2014, http://www .ft.com/cms/s/0/d123d896-5808-11e4-b47d-00144feab7de .html; Richard Wong, "The Roots of Hong Kong's Income Inequality," *South China Morning Post*, April 28, 2015, http://

www.scmp.com/business/global-economy/article/1752277
/roots-hong-kongs-income-inequality.

76. Liyan Chen, "Beyond the Umbrella Movement: Hong Kong's
Struggle with Inequality in 8 Charts," *Forbes,* October 8, 2014,
http://www.forbes.com/sites/liyanchen/2014/10/08/beyond
-the-umbrella-revolution-hong-kongs-struggle-with-inequality
-in-8-charts/#5cc54fc550b6.

77. Adam Connors, "Hong Kong's Umbrella Movement: A Timeline
of Key Events One Year On," *ABC,* September 27, 2015, http://
www.abc.net.au/news/2015-09-28/timeline-hong-kong
-umbrella-movement-one-year-on/6802388.

78. Chloe Pantaz, "The 15 Most Expensive Cities in the World for
Renters," *Business Insider,* April 22, 2016, http://www
.businessinsider.com/most-expensive-cities-for-renters-2016
-4?r=UK&IR=T;.

79. In 2013, the average monthly salary of a recent college graduate
was only HK$10,860; in 1993, average monthly salary was
HK$13,158 (Phila Siu, "Salaries of Hong Kong's University
Graduates Dropped 20 Per Cent in Last 20 Years, Study Finds,"
South China Morning Post, July 29, 2015, http://www.scmp
.com/news/hong-kong/economy/article/1844661/salaries-hong
-kongs-university-graduates-dropped-20-cent-last?page=all;
Susie Poppick, "Here's What the Average Grad Makes Right Out
of College," *Time,* April 22, 2015, http://time.com/money
/3829776/heres-what-the-average-grad-makes-right-out-of
-college/).

80. In 1993, the average monthly salary was HK$13,158. (Phila Siu,
"Salaries of Hong Kong's University Graduates Dropped 20 Per
Cent in Last 20 Years, Study Finds," *South China Morning Post,*
July 29, 2015, http://www.scmp.com/news/hong-kong
/economy/article/1844661/salaries-hong-kongs-university
-graduates-dropped-20-cent-last?page=all).

81. UBS, "Prices & Earnings," UBS Switzerland AG, September 17,
2015, 13, https://www.ubs.com /microsites/prices-earnings
/prices-earnings.html.

82. Thomas Zhang, "Burned Out Junior Bankers in Hong Kong Start
Looking for an Escape Route," efinancialcareers, February 24,
2015, http://news.efinancialcareers.com/uk-en/199632
/burned-junior-bankers-hong-kong-start-looking-escape-route/.

83. Maya Kosoff, "This Chinese Messaging App is Taking the Country by Storm—and Facebook Should Pay Attention," *Business Insider,* August 10, 2015, http://www.businessinsider.com /wechat-why-it-dominates-china-2015-8.

84. Carol Giacomo, "In Rural India, Hoping for Jobs and Education in a Growing Economy," *New York Times,* March 16, 2015, http:// www.nytimes.com/2015/03/16/opinion/in-rural-india-hoping -for-jobs-and-education-in-a-growing-economy.html?r=1.

85. By 2020, 40 percent of college graduates from G20 and OECD countries will be from China and India alone. By contrast, the United States and European Union countries are expected to account for just over a quarter of young people with tertiary degrees (Organization for Economic Co-operation and Development, *Education Indicators in Focus* (Paris: OECD Publishing, May 2012), 1, http://www .oecd.org/edu/50495363.pdf).

86. Manjeet Kripalani and Pete Engardio with Steve Hamm, "The Rise of India," *Bloomberg,* December 8, 2003, http://www .bloomberg.com/news/articles/2003-12-07/the-rise-of-india.

87. Sylvia Vorhauser-Smith, "Opportunity Is Knocking in Southeast Asia—Can You Hear It?," *Forbes,* March 7, 2014, http://www .forbes.com/sites/sylviavorhausersmith/2014/03/07/opportunity -is-knocking-in-southeast-asia-can-you-hear-it/#477a20f13fda; Chris Schnabel, "Philippine GDP Grows 6.3% in Q4 2015," *Rappler,* January 28, 2016, http://www.rappler.com/business /economy-watch/120543-philippines-gross-domestic-product-2015.

88. "Where Do the Most OFW Remittances Come From?" *iMoney Philippines,* June 9, 2015, http://www.imoney.ph/articles/ofw -remittances-philippines-infographic/; "Infographic: Where $26.92B of OFW Remittances Come From," GMA News Online, June 9, 2015, http://www.gmanetwork.com/news/story /500918/money/infographic-where-26-92b-of-ofw-remittances -come-from.

89. A recent study conducted by the Far Eastern University Policy Center found that 21.3 percent of college freshmen have fathers working overseas (Earl Victor L. Rosero, "Who Is the Filipino Millennial? Most College Freshmen Want to Work Abroad, Take Graduate Studies, Care about the Environment," *GMA News Online,* August 8, 2015, http://www.gmanetwork.com/news /story/532123/lifestyle /artandculture/most-college-freshmen

-want-to-work-abroad-take-graduate-studies-care-about-the
-environment #sthash.Pz8bJENt.dpuf).

90. "Decoding Millennials," Philippine Association of National
    Advertisers, accessed May 11, 2016, http://pana.com.ph
    /decoding-Millennials/.

91. Leong Chee Tung, "Singapore at 50: Population Pressure and
    the War for Talent," *Gallup*, August 24, 2015, http://www
    .gallup.com/businessjournal/184736/singapore-population
    -pressure-war-talent.aspx; LinkedIn and Ipsos, "The Affluent
    Millennial Opportunity: Singapore," LinkedIn, June, 2015, 2,
    https:// business.linkedin.com/content/dam/business
    /marketing-solutions/global/en_US/campaigns/pdfs/2015
    %20Singapore%20Affluent%20Millennials%20Research%20Study
    .pdf; National Population and Talent Division, Prime Minister's
    Office, Singapore Department of Statistics, Ministry of Home
    Affairs, and Immigration and Checkpoints Authority, *Population
    in Brief 2015* (Government of Singapore, September 2015),
    17, http://www.nptd.gov.sg/Portals/0/Homepage/Highlights/
    population
    -in-brief-2015.pdf.

92. NPTD et al., *Population in Brief 2015* (see note 93).

93. Chee Tung, "Singapore at 50," http://www.gallup.com
    /businessjournal/184736/singapore-population-pressure-war
    -talent.aspx; Michelle Price, "Singapore Talent War Intensifies
    as Immigration Curbs Kick In," *Financial News*, April 3, 2014,
    http://www.efinancialnews.com/story/2014-04-03/singapore
    -talent-war-intensifies-as-immigration-curbs-kick-in.

94. Sarah Murray, "Volunteering at Work Makes Sound Business
    Sense," *Financial Times*, February 26, 2016, http://www
    .ft.com/cms/s/0/609e1040-d0b2-11e5-92a1-c5e23ef99c77
    .html#axzz42KIG2cFm.

95. Ibid.

96. "Accenture Development Partnerships," Accenture, 2013,
    https://www.accenture.com/us-en/~/media/Accenture
    /Conversion-Assets/DotCom/Documents/Global/PDF/Strategy
    _5/Accenture-FINAL-10-Year-Infographic-May-2013-FINAL.pdf.

97. "Accenture Development Partnerships in Partnership with
    Oxfam," Accenture, 2007, http://www.bitc.org.uk/sites/default

/files/kcfinder/files/Accenture_and_Oxfam_-_Sustainable
_Livelihoods.pdf.

98. Murray, "Volunteering at Work" (see note 106).

99. "Accenture Development Partnerships" (see note 108).

100. Max Nisen, "Why GE Had to Kill Its Annual Performance Reviews after More than Three Decades," *Quartz*, August 13, 2015, http://qz.com/428813/ge-performance-review-strategy-shift/.

101. Shareen Pathak, "How PepsiCo Sweetens Up Consumer Insights," Digiday, June 8, 2015, http://digiday.com/brands /pepsico-sweetens-consumer-insights/.

METHODOLOGY

The research consists of a survey, Insights In-Depth® sessions (a proprietary web-based tool used to conduct voice-facilitated virtual focus groups) involving more than one hundred people from our Task Force organizations, and one-on-one interviews with fifty-seven men and women in the US, Brazil, China, Hong Kong, India, the Philippines, Singapore, and the UK.

The US survey was conducted online between June 2014 and August 2014 among 3,298 respondents between the ages of twenty-one and sixty-four currently employed in certain white-collar occupations, with at least a bachelor's degree; 765 of these respondents are Millennials, born in 1982 or later. A follow up survey was conducted online in January 2016 among 291 Millennial respondents from the first survey. Data in the US were weighted to be representative of the US population on key demographics (age, gender, race/ethnicity, region, education, and income). The base used for statistical testing was the effective base.

The multimarket survey comes from three large-scale samples of 11,936 respondents over the age of twenty-one currently employed full-time, with at least a bachelor's degree. Survey 1, conducted online between November 2014 and April 2015, includes 5,018 respondents (1,005 in Brazil; 1,005 in China; 1,001 in Hong Kong; 1,004 in India; and 1,003 in the UK), of which 2,006 are Millennials. Survey 2, conducted online in May 2015, includes 5,013 respondents (1,007 in Brazil, 1,001 in China, 1,001 in Hong Kong, 1,000 in India, and 1,004 in the UK), of which 1,790 are Millennials. Survey 3, conducted between February 2016 and March 2016, includes 947 respondents in the Philippines (including 440 Millennials) and 958 in Singapore (including 410 Millennials). Data in all surveys were weighted on age and gender. The base used for statistical testing was the effective base.

The US surveys were conducted by Knowledge Networks under the auspices of the Center for Talent Innovation, a nonprofit research organization. The multimarket survey was conducted by GMI Lightspeed under the auspices of the Center for Talent Innovation. Knowledge Networks and GMI Lightspeed were responsible for the data collection, while the Center for Talent Innovation conducted the analysis.

In the charts, percentages may not always add up to 100 because of computer rounding or the acceptance of multiple responses from respondents.

ACKNOWLEDGMENTS

The authors are deeply grateful to the study sponsors and those who have been integral to the research's success—Colleen Dwyer, Jocelyn Seidenfeld, Nancy Testa, and Karrie Wang at American Express; Crystal Andrews and Linda Hartman-Reehl at Baxalta; Yvonne Breitenfeld, Diana Cruz Solash, Karyn Twaronite, and Mac Worsham at EY; Sandra Altine, Frances G. Laserson, Jennifer Rivera, and Sara Weil at The Moody's Foundation; Barbara Keen, Lisa Le Vere, and Jackie Scanlan at Novo Nordisk; and Alice Avellanet and Rosemarie Lanard at S&P Global—for their generous support. We would also like to thank the cochairs of the Task Force for Talent Innovation—Redia Anderson, Cynthia Bowman, Erika Irish Brown, Deb Bubb, Yrthya Dinzey-Flores, Deborah Elam, Gail Fierstein, Cassandra Frangos, Trevor Gandy, David Gonzales, Wanda Hope, Rosalind Hudnell, Renee Johnson, Patricia Langer, Kate Nekic-Padgett, Kendall O'Brien, Lisa Garcia Quiroz, Craig Robinson, Shari Slate, David Tamburelli, Eileen Taylor, Anré Williams, and Melinda Wolfe—for their vision and commitment.

We deeply appreciate the efforts of the CTI team, specifically Noni Allwood, Justin Bilyeu, Joseph

Cervone, Diana Forster, Kennedy Ihezie, Julia Taylor Kennedy, and Peggy Shiller. Thanks also to Terri Chung, Danielle Cruz, Colin Elliott, Mark Fernandez, Jessica Jia, Lawrence Jones, Carolyn Buck Luce, Deidra Mascoll, Becky Midura, Andrea Turner Moffitt, Ripa Rashid, Brandon Urquhart, and Eunice Yu for their support. We also appreciate the support provided by our interns Roxanna Azari and Thomas Tuthill.

Thanks also to the rest of the private sector members of the Task Force for Talent Innovation for their practical ideas and collaborative energy: Elaine Aarons, Rachael Akohonae, Jennifer Allyn, Rohini Anand, Jolen Anderson, Michelle Angier, Diane Ashley, Nadine Augusta, Jane Ayaduray, Ken Barrett, Myrna Chao, Kenneth Charles, Jyoti Chopra, Elise Clarke, Janessa Cox, Nancy Di Dia, Miriam Donaldson, Nicole Erb, Hedieh Fakhriyazdi, Grace Figueredo, Kent Gardiner, Heide Gardner, Robert Gottlieb, Marc Grainger, Kavita Gupta, Lisa Gutierrez, Kathleen Hart, Neesha Hathi, Maja Hazell, Jessica Heffron, Kara Helander, Celia Pohani Huber, Bill Huffaker, Sylvia James, Panagiotis (Pete) Karahalios, Shannon Kelleher, Janice Little, Cynthia Marshall, Beth McCormick, Mark McLane, Piyush Mehta, Sylvester Mendoza, Michele Meyer-Shipp, Carolanne Minashi, Kristen Mleczko, Loren Monroe-Trice, Meredith Moore, Christal Morris, Tricia Myers, Janell Nelson, Birgit Neu, Elizabeth Nieto, Pamela Norley, Jennifer O'Lear, Adebola Osakwe, Cindy Pace, Monica Parham, Jimmie Paschall, Cara

Peck, Donna Pedro, LaTonia Pouncey, Danyale Price, Susan Reid, Eiry Roberts, Dwight Robinson, Christine Rogers-Raetsch, Deborah Rosado Shaw, Aida Sabo, Meisha Sherman, Ellyn Shook, Maria Stolfi, Karen Sumberg, Brian Tippens, NV "Tiger" Tyagarajan, Vera Vitels, Lynn O'Connor Vos, Barbara Wankoff, Jennifer Welty, Nadia Younes, and Charles Yost.

Thanks also to Serge Agroskin, Andy Ajello, Justin Angelle, Maurizio Asperti, Anne Bodnar, Connie Bustamante, Lynne Coviello, Mike Dill, Julius Dunn, Leida Ferguson, Maryella Gockel, Sarah Goodwin, Brendan Greenfield-Turk, Alexandra Hille, Courtney Keplinger, Ibi Krukrubo, Tiphany Lee-Allen, Erica Lynam, Shane Mullin, Niki Patel, Thinette Quilaneta, Karthik R, Tierra Ryan, Aline Santos, Mohit Saxena, Vikram Singh, Rana Strellis, Adonis Watkins, Lisa Westlake, Vanessa Youngs, and the women and men who took part in focus groups and Insights In-Depth® sessions.

ADDITIONAL PUBLICATIONS

KEEPING TALENTED WOMEN ON THE ROAD TO SUCCESS

Ambition in Black and White: The Feminist Narrative, Revised
Center for Talent Innovation, June 2016

The Power of the Purse: Engaging Women Decision Makers for Healthy Outcomes
Sponsors: Aetna, Bristol-Myers Squibb, Cardinal Health, Eli Lilly and Company, Johnson & Johnson, Merck & Co., Merck KGaA, MetLife, Pfizer, PwC, Strategy&, Teva, WPP (2015)

Women Want Five Things
Sponsors: American Express, AT&T, Bank of America, Boehringer Ingelheim USA, Merck KGaA, The Moody's Foundation (2014)

Harnessing the Power of the Purse: Female Investors and Global Opportunities for Growth
Sponsors: Credit Suisse, Deutsche Bank, Goldman Sachs, Morgan Stanley, Standard Chartered Bank, UBS (2014)

Executive Presence: The Missing Link between Merit and Success
HarperCollins, June 2014

Forget a Mentor, Find a Sponsor: The New Way to Fast-Track Your Career
Harvard Business Review Press, September 2013

On-Ramps and Up-Ramps India
Sponsors: Citi, Genpact, Sodexo, Standard Chartered Bank,
Unilever (2013)

Executive Presence
Sponsors: American Express, Bloomberg LP, Credit Suisse,
Ernst & Young, Gap Inc., Goldman Sachs, Interpublic Group,
The Moody's Foundation (2012)

Sponsor Effect 2.0: Road Maps for Sponsors and Protégés
Sponsors: American Express, AT&T, Booz Allen Hamilton,
Deloitte, Freddie Mac, Genentech, Morgan Stanley (2012)

Sponsor Effect: UK
Sponsor: Lloyds Banking Group (2012)

**Off-Ramps and On-Ramps Japan: Keeping Talented Women
on the Road to Success**
Sponsors: Bank of America, Cisco, Goldman Sachs (2011)

The Relationship You Need to Get Right
Harvard Business Review, October 2011

Sponsor Effect: Breaking Through the Last Glass Ceiling
Sponsors: American Express, Deloitte, Intel, Morgan Stanley
(2010)

Off-Ramps and On-Ramps Revisited
Harvard Business Review, June 2010

Off-Ramps and On-Ramps Revisited
Sponsors: Cisco, Ernst & Young, The Moody's Foundation
(2010)

Letzte Ausfahrt Babypause
Harvard Business Manager (Germany), May 2010

Off-Ramps and On-Ramps Germany
Sponsors: Boehringer Ingelheim, Deutsche Bank, Siemens AG
(2010)

*Off-Ramps and On-Ramps: Keeping Talented Women on the
Road to Success*
Harvard Business Review Press, 2007

*Off-Ramps and On-Ramps: Keeping Talented Women on the
Road to Success*
Harvard Business Review, March 2005

*The Hidden Brain Drain: Off-Ramps and On-Ramps in
Women's Careers*
Sponsors: Ernst & Young, Goldman Sachs, Lehman Brothers
(2005)

LEVERAGING MINORITY AND MULTICULTURAL TALENT

Black Women: Ready to Lead
Sponsors: American Express, AT&T, Bank of America, Chubb
Group of Insurance Companies, The Depository Trust &
Clearing Corporation, Intel, Morgan Stanley, White & Case
LLP (2015)

*How Diversity Drives Innovation: A Compendium of Best
Practices*
Sponsors: Bloomberg LP, Bristol-Myers Squibb, Cisco,
Deutsche Bank, EY, Siemens AG, Time Warner (2014)

*Cracking the Code: Executive Presence and Multicultural
Professionals*
Sponsors: Bank of America, Chubb Group of Insurance
Companies, Deloitte, GE, Intel Corporation, McKesson
Corporation (2013)

How Diversity Can Drive Innovation
Harvard Business Review, December 2013

Innovation, Diversity and Market Growth
Sponsors: Bloomberg LP, Bristol-Myers Squibb, Cisco,
Deutsche Bank, EY, Siemens AG, Time Warner (2013)

Vaulting the Color Bar: How Sponsorship Levers
Multicultural Professionals into Leadership
Sponsors: American Express, Bank of America, Bristol-Myers
Squibb, Deloitte, Intel, Morgan Stanley, NBCUniversal (2012)

Asians in America: Unleashing the Potential of the "Model
Minority"
Sponsors: Deloitte, Goldman Sachs, Pfizer, Time Warner (2011)

Sin Fronteras: Celebrating and Capitalizing on the Strengths
of Latina Executives
Sponsors: Booz Allen Hamilton, Cisco, Credit Suisse, General
Electric, Goldman Sachs, Johnson & Johnson, Time Warner
(2007)

Global Multicultural Executives and the Talent Pipeline
Sponsors: Citigroup, General Electric, PepsiCo, Time Warner,
Unilever (2008)

Leadership in Your Midst: Tapping the Hidden Strengths of
Minority Executives
Harvard Business Review, November 2005

Invisible Lives: Celebrating and Leveraging Diversity in the
Executive Suite
Sponsors: General Electric, Time Warner, Unilever (2005)

Forthcoming 2016: Culture Smarts: Maximizing the
Potential of Latino Talent

REALIZING THE FULL POTENTIAL OF LGBT TALENT

Out in the World: Securing LGBT Rights in the Global Marketplace
Sponsors: American Express, Bank of America, Barclays, Bloomberg LP, BNY Mellon, BP, Chubb Group of Insurance Companies, Deutsche Bank, Eli Lilly and Company, Ernst & Young LLP, and Out Leadership (2016)

The Power of "Out" 2.0: LGBT in the Workplace
Sponsors: Deloitte, Out on the Street, Time Warner (2013)

For LGBT Workers, Being "Out" Brings Advantages
Harvard Business Review, July/August 2011

The Power of "Out": LGBT in the Workplace
Sponsors: American Express, Boehringer Ingelheim USA, Cisco, Credit Suisse, Deloitte, Google (2011)

RETAINING AND SUSTAINING TOP TALENT

Mission Critical: Unlocking the Value of Vets in the Workforce
Sponsors: Booz Allen Hamilton, Boehringer Ingelheim USA, Fordham University, Intercontinental Exchange/NYSE, Prudential Financial, The Moody's Foundation, Wounded Warrior Project (2015)

Top Talent: Keeping Performance Up When Business Is Down
Harvard Business Press, 2009

Sustaining High Performance in Difficult Times
Sponsor: The Moody's Foundation (2008)

Seduction and Risk: The Emergence of Extreme Jobs
Sponsors: American Express, BP plc, ProLogis, UBS (2007)

Extreme Jobs: The Dangerous Allure of the 70-Hour Workweek
Harvard Business Review, December 2006

Forthcoming 2017: **Disrupting Bias, Uncovering Value**

TAPPING INTO THE STRENGTHS OF GEN Y, GEN X, AND BOOMERS

The X Factor: Tapping into the Strengths of the 33- to 46-Year-Old Generation
Sponsors: American Express, Boehringer Ingelheim USA, Cisco, Credit Suisse, Google (2011)

How Gen Y & Boomers Will Reshape Your Agenda
Harvard Business Review, July/August 2009

Bookend Generations: Leveraging Talent and Finding Common Ground
Sponsors: Booz Allen Hamilton, Ernst & Young, Lehman Brothers, Time Warner, UBS (2009)

BECOMING A TALENT MAGNET IN EMERGING MARKETS

Growing Global Executives: The New Competencies
Sponsors: American Express, Bloomberg LP, Cisco Systems, EY, Genpact, Goldman Sachs, Intel, Pearson, Sodexo, The Moody's Foundation (2015)

The Battle for Female Talent in Brazil
Sponsors: Bloomberg LP, Booz & Company, Intel, Pfizer, Siemens AG (2011)

Winning the War for Talent in Emerging Markets
Harvard Business Press, August 2011

The Battle for Female Talent in China
Sponsors: Bloomberg LP, Booz & Company, Intel, Pfizer, Siemens AG (2010)

The Battle for Female Talent in India
Sponsors: Bloomberg LP, Booz & Company, Intel, Pfizer, Siemens AG (2010)

The Battle for Female Talent in Emerging Markets
Harvard Business Review, May 2010

PREVENTING THE EXODUS OF WOMEN IN SET

Athena Factor 2.0: Accelerating Female Talent in Science, Engineering & Technology
Sponsors: American Express, Boehringer Ingelheim USA, BP, Genentech, McKesson Corporation, Merck Serono, Schlumberger, Siemens AG (2014)

The Under-Leveraged Talent Pool: Women Technologists on Wall Street
Sponsors: Bank of America, Credit Suisse, Goldman Sachs, Intel, Merrill Lynch, NYSE Euronext (2008)

Stopping the Exodus of Women in Science
Harvard Business Review, June 2008

The Athena Factor: Reversing the Brain Drain in Science, Engineering, and Technology
Sponsors: Alcoa, Cisco, Johnson & Johnson, Microsoft, Pfizer (2008)

TASK FORCE FOR TALENT INNOVATION

Hewlett-Packard

HSBC Bank plc

International Monetary Fund

Interpublic Group

Intuit

Kohlberg Kravis Roberts

KPMG LLP

L-3

McKesson Corporation

McKinsey & Company

Merck*

MetLife

Microsoft

The Moody's Foundation**

Morgan Stanley

Northrop Grumman

Novartis Pharmaceuticals Corp.

Novo Nordisk

Ogilvy & Mather

PAREXEL International

Paul, Weiss, Rifkind, Wharton & Garrison LLP

PepsiCo

Pfizer Inc.**

Pratt & Whitney

Prudential Financial

PwC

QBE North America

S&P Global

Sodexo

Standard Chartered Bank

Swiss Reinsurance Co.

Thomson Reuters

UBS**

Vanguard

Visa

Weil, Gotshal & Manges LLP

Wells Fargo and Company

White & Case LLP

Willis Towers Watson

Withers LLP

WPP

* Merck KGaA (Darmstadt, Germany)
** Steering Committee

As of June 1, 2016

INDEX

Symbols

91%. *See* Ninety-One Percent

A

Accenture Development Partnerships 123–125
ADP. *See* Accenture Development Partnership
affirmative action 44
Agroskin, Serge 83–84, 86
Ajello, Andy 45–47
ambition 28, 41, 73–77, 79–80, 107
American Express 6, 61, 92
Angelle, Justin 60
Argentina 66
Asia 31, 91–92, 115
AsiaPac. *See* Asia-Pacific
Asia-Pacific 29, 91–93
Atlantic 80

B

Baby Boomer xv, 4–6, 15, 20, 42, 45, 54, 73, 86, 90, 96, 124,
  126–127
balinghou 96
Baxalta 68, 106, 125–126; Dress for your Day 126
BBBS. *See* Big Brothers Big Sisters
Big Brothers Big Sisters 131–133
Bookend Generations 73
Brazil 12, 61–63, 66; economic expansion 63
Bulloch, Gib 123–124

C

career counselor 39–40
Census 5
Center for Talent Innovation vi, xv, 24, 29, 41, 43, 73
Chicago 125–126
China 12, 91–93, 95–96

coaching 130; career 47; on-the-job 57
confidence gap 76
cost of living; Hong Kong 99; UK 69; Philippines 110
Cruz Solash, Diana 57, 61
CTI. *See* Center for Talent Innovation

D

Dill, Mike 134
Dimon, Jamie 20
diversity; acquired 25; among US Millennials 5, 12, 23–25;
  inherent 24–25; two-dimensional 25
dotcom bubble 54

E

ERG. *See* Novo Nordisk; Millennial Employee Resource Group
EY 55–57, 61, 127–129; Applause Awards 57; flexibility 127

F

Facebook 59, 64, 104
face time 102; lack of 65, 95
feedback 21, 45, 47, 56–57, 61, 65, 126, 129–130, 139
financial privilege 14–15, 19, 29–31, 33, 37, 43, 49, 50, 59–60,
  74, 85
Financial Times 91, 123
flexible work arrangement 37–38, 127, 128
Forbes 55
Fortune 500 91
FWA. *See* flexible work arrangement

G

GDP. *See* gross domestic product
GE. *See* General Electric
General Electric 129–131; the vitality curve 129
Generation Me 10
Generation X xv, 4–5, 9, 15, 20, 42, 45, 62, 73, 86, 90, 126
Generation Y 4, 61, 63–66
Generation Z 136–137
Gini coefficient 14

Global Generations 127
Gockel, Maryella 127–129
Goodwin, Sarah 68
Google 70, 103
Great Recession, the 6
gross domestic product 91, 100, 111, 115
Guardian xiii
Gvillo, Stefania 135–137

H

Hartman-Reehl, Linda 125–127
Hewlett Consulting Partners xv
Hewlett, Sylvia Ann viii
high compensation 49, 53, 55, 62, 98–99
Hille, Alexandra 40–43
Hong Kong 12, 93, 99–103

I

India 12, 92–93, 105–107; social movements 107
inequality; Hong Kong 99; Singapore 116–118; UK 69; US
    xiv, 5–6, 14
intellectual growth xvi, 19, 23, 27, 29–33, 70, 87–88, 107, 110
international experience 33–34

J

Jiménez, Marcus 137
job insecurity 29
JP Morgan 20

K

Kay, Katty 76
Keen, Barbara 8, 21–22
Krishnamoorthy, Raghu 131
Krukrubo, Ibi 55–56

L

Lanard, Rosemarie 75, 84
Latin America 33–34, 92

leadership; gap 4; homogeneous 24; inclusive behavior xvi; Millennials as bench strength xv, 7; potential 7, 55, 86, 88, 95; skills 39
Lean In 73, 76
Lee-Allen, Tiphany 131, 133
Lewis, Rob 138–140
LGBT xvi, 5, 38, 107

M

meaning and purpose 9, 49–51, 70, 123–124
mentor 21, 28–29, 39, 47, 52, 75, 112, 131–133, 135; mentor program 28, 131–132
methodology 12, 155–156; multimarket survey 92–93, 155–156; US survey 13–14, 155–156
Millennials; Brazil 61–65; China 93, 95–96, 98; consumer market 6–7; flight risk 11, 13, 19, 65; Hong Kong 99, 103; India 105–108; of color 11, 22–23, 43, 45, 131; older 83–87, 89–90; Philippines 110–113; Singapore 115–116, 118; spending power 6; stereotypes xiv, 10–11, 15, 49, 56, 60, 62, 66, 93, 107, 109; UK 66–67; women 10, 71–76, 78–80
MNC. *See* multinational corporations
Moody's 21, 27–28, 37, 50–51, 56, 75, 83–84, 131–133; Bridging the Gap Workplace Mentorship 131–133
mortgage crisis 54
multinational corporations 92, 101, 107, 110, 113, 116, Murad, Ezra 124
My Brother's Keeper 131

N

News America Marketing 40
Ninety-One Percent 15, 31, 39, 49, 53, 60, 84
Noordende, Sander van't 124
Novo Nordisk 8, 21, 45–47, 51–52, 60, 133–135; Idea Stream Project 52; Millennial Employee Resource Group 131, 133–135; Take Action Challenge 52

O

Obama, Barack 131
Occupy Wall Street 5
Oxfam 124

P

Patel, Niki 51–52
PD@GE. *See* Performance Development at GE
PepsiCo 135–137; Insights Data App 135–136
Performance Development at GE 129–130
Peters, Susan 129–130
Pfizer 137–139; Talent Marketplace 137–139
Philippines 12, 93, 103, 109–112; languages spoken 112
Politico 20
post-racial 11
professional development 27–28, 47, 77

Q

quality of life 66, 68, 70, 99, 101–102, 109
Quilaneta, Thinette 109–110

R

recognition 10, 45, 49, 56–57, 59–62, 95, 102, 107, 124
relationship capital 75
rewarding relationships xvi, 19, 23, 37, 56, 87, 89, 112
Ryan, Tierra 139

S

Sandberg, Sheryl 72
Sanders, Bernie 14
Santos, Aline 65
Saxena, Mohit 106–107
Scanlan, Jackie 134–135
Science, Engineering, and Technology (SET) 79; women 79
Shipman, Claire 76
Singapore 12, 93, 115–119; expatriate dominance 116
skills; language 25, 32; leadership 39
Slaughter, Anne-Marie 80
social media 61, 64–65, 73, 103–104, 118
speak-up culture 25
S&P Global 65, 75, 84, 109–110
sponsorship 29, 40–42, 89–90, 113, 133; people of color 24, 43–45; sponsor xv, 21, 41–45, 134; sponsor effect 41; women 41

student loans 54–55

T

Testa, Nancy 6, 61, 92
The Confidence Code: The Science and Art of Self-Assurance—What Women Should Know 76
the sponsor effect 41
training 112; customer 7–8; employee 7–9, 20, 47, 87; IT 103; lack of 12, 24, 92; language 33, 113; leadership 88; on-the-job 7–8; personnel management 88; program 30, 88, 132
Trump, Donald 14
Twenge, Jean 10

U

Umbrella Movement, the 100
unconscious bias 44
United Kingdom xiv, 12, 66–70, 110, 117
United States vi, xiv, 5, 12–13, 24, 30, 34, 55, 91–93, 100, 103, 106–107, 111; millennial demographics xvi, 3–4, 9, 125, 129, 131

V

Vaulting the Color Bar 44

W

Wall Street 15, 27
Wall Street Journal 92
Watkins, Adonis 27–29
wealth gap 5, 14
Weil, Sara 50–51
Welch, Jack 129
WEN. *See* Women's Empowerment Network
Westlake, Lisa 21, 37–38, 56, 75–76
Women's Empowerment Network; Women's Conference 74
Women Want Five Things 74
work-life balance 66, 68, 101, 103
World Trade Center 54

Y

YOLO/You only live once 53
Youngs, Vanessa 132

ABOUT THE AUTHORS

Joan Snyder Kuhl is a fellow for CTI and principal of HCP. Kuhl has thirteen years of corporate management experience working at Eli Lilly, Forest Laboratories, and Actavis in sales, marketing, organizational effectiveness, training, and development. She is an international speaker and Founder of Why Millennials Matter, a research and consulting agency. She is coauthor of two books: *The First Globals: Understanding, Managing and Unleashing the Potential of our Millennial Generation*; and *Peter Drucker's Five Most Important Questions: Enduring Wisdom for Today's Leaders.* She serves on the *Cosmopolitan Magazine* Millennial Advisory Board and at The Frances Hesselbein Leadership Institute. As the career expert for Barnes & Noble College (BNC), Kuhl speaks on campus and at conferences and provides live and digital content for the 5.2 million students associated with their 725+ stores. She shares research and advice on success strategies for transitioning from college to career. She earned her BSBA from The University of Pittsburgh and an MBA from Rutgers University.

Jennifer Zephirin is senior vice president of strategic outreach at the Center for Talent Innovation. Prior to joining CTI, Zephirin was a diversity and inclusion manager for Morgan Stanley where she specialized in organizational culture change management, pipeline development, employee resource group management, and retention of high-potential mid- to senior-level employees, with a focus on women in both Wealth Management and Institution Securities. Previously, she held positions as a compensation and recruiting associate for NERA Economic Consulting and as a consultant with FactSet Research in the Investment Management division. Zephirin received a BA in Economics from Fairfield University.